THE PRISONER'S SILENCE

THE PRISONER'S SILENCE

VARGHESE V DEVASIA

WhiteFalcon
Publishing

www.whitefalconpublishing.com

The Prisoner's Silence
Varghese V Devasia

www.whitefalconpublishing.com

To

The nameless, voiceless and friendless convicts hanged
on the crossbar for the crimes of others.

A meditation on human existence, *The Prisoner's Silence* highlights the scary face of the law, politics, religion, and God, the primary subjugation sources leading to the gallows. Power, human or divine, emerges from violence and submission, flourishes with flattery, and acquires sanctity through servility. Profoundly philosophical, incisively psychological, enticingly humane, and universally sociological, the novel is a nutshell of humanity's bondage, conflicts, alienation and anticipation.

Jose Luke, Kolkata.

The Prisoner's Silence is an existential, intersubjective novel about two convicts condemned to death, but both confronted God.

Thoma Kunj was innocent, an ontological contradiction of being human. Denied fundamental rights, he realised those rights were for the powerful, rich and influential. He was afraid and ignorant of the law and kept a profound silence in the court, prison and on the gallows, as he was alone.

Razak, too, was alone. When thirteen, he ran away from Kerala and was castrated by Muhammad Akeem, a dates palm planter in an oasis in Saudi Arabia, to serve in Akeem's harem. Razak escaped after nineteen years of terror and returned to his native village. His greatest disappointment was that he could not save a Pakistani girl, Amira, eleven years when he first met her in the zenana. They loved each other and wanted to escape and live together. Even though unable to have sex, he longed for companionship with Amira, and she was willing. In Ponnani, Razak married a girl from Calicut, hiding the fact that he was impotent. He killed his wife and her paramour with a Malappuram sword within a year.

Razak questioned Allah why did he allow Muhammad Akeem to castrate him. He wanted revenge on Akeem and Allah; the only option was to evolve like Akeem. At the gallows, the masked Thoma Kunj heard the feeble cry of Razak, the anguish of humanity, but a fearless challenge to Allah.

About the Author

Varghese V Devasia is a former Professor and Dean at Tata Institute of Social Sciences and the Head of the Tata Institute of Social Sciences Tuljapur Campus. He was a Professor and Principal at MSS Institute of Social Work, Nagpur University, Nagpur.

He researched a Borstal School attached to the Central Prison Kannur for his MA, specialising in Criminology and Correctional Administration at Tata Institute of Social Sciences, Mumbai. For his LLB, he concentrated on criminal law; his MPhil thesis was on criminal homicide. He studied 220 convicted murderers in Central Prison Nagpur at Nagpur University for his doctorate. He gained a Diploma in Human Rights Law from the National School of India University, Bengaluru, and a Certificate of Achievement in Justice from Harvard University.

The Ministry of Home Affairs, Government of India, published some of his seminal research studies such as *Sexual Behaviour of Male Prison Inmates in Criminal Homicide, Victim Offender Association and Interaction in Criminal Homicide,* and *The Phenomenon of Criminal*

Homicide in its Indian Journal of Criminology and Criminalistics. His article *Victim Offender Relationship in Female Homicide by Male*, published in the Indian Journal of Social Work, is a widely cited research paper. He has published about ten academic reference books in Criminology, Correctional Administration, Victimology and Human Rights.

He has authored an anthology of short stories, *A Woman with Large Eyes*, published by Olympia Publishers, London. He is the recipient of the Author of the Year for Fiction Award for his debut novel, *Women of God's Own Country*, published by Book Solutions Indulekha Media Network, Kottayam, conferred by Ukiyoto Publishing. Ukiyoto Publishing published his novels, *The Celibate* and *Amaya The Buddha*. He is the author of a Malayalam novelette, *Daivathinte Manasum Kurishuthakarthavate Koodavum*, published by Mulberry Publishers, Calicut. He lives in Kozhikode, Kerala.

Email: vvdevasia@gmail.com

Acknowledgements

My inspiration for writing this novel sprouted when I researched two hundred and twenty lifer convicts in Central Prison, Nagpur. It was a painful realisation that some of them hadn't committed the crime they were accused of, thus leaving their families and undergoing incarceration subjected them to untold miseries. The prison officials knew that a couple of prisoners hanged on the gallows were innocents and died for someone else's crime; therefore, they lost their right to live due to deceit. They were the voiceless and forgotten individuals in society, mainly Adivasis, Dalits, and minorities. So, to a large extent, the criminal justice system in India remained a hoax. Two convicts I met at the Central Prison, Kannur, forced me to rewrite what I learned about the Indian Penal Code, Criminal Procedure Code and Evidence Act.

I have visited almost all prisons in Maharashtra, some in Kerala, Tihar in Delhi and a few in Tamil Nadu and Andhra Pradesh. I am grateful to the prison officers for making arrangements so that I could meet the lifer convicts in those prisons.

Jills Varghese, a person with a refined sense of aesthetics and justice, read the manuscript; I am grateful for his scholarly and philosophical comments. I am indebted to Jose Luke for his valued overview. Shrimayee Thakur of White Falcon Publishing has done a splendid job editing the book; I am thankful to her.

Contents

Glossary

1. Abaya (Arabic): A robe-like dress worn by women in the Arab world.
2. Al-jahim (Arabic): Hell.
3. Arak (Arabic): A distilled alcohol.
4. Akki Otti (Kodagu): Unleavened flatbread of cooked rice and rice flour.
5. Bahiya (Arabic): A gorgeous girl.
6. Chemmeen (Malayalam): A famous Malayalam novel by Thakazi, and a Malayalam movie of the same name.
7. Gharara (Hindi/Urdu): A traditional dress worn by women in India and Pakistan.
8. Gursan (Arabic): A thin bread with meat.
9. Haram (Arabic): Forbidden.
10. Harem (Arabic): A house for the concubines of a polygamous man.
11. Houri (Arabic): A virgin who awaits the faithful male believer in paradise.
12. Iblis (Arabic): Leader of devils.
13. Jahannam (Arabic): Hell.
14. Jalamah (Arabic): A dish of lamb meat.

15. Jannah (Arabic): Paradise, Heaven.
16. Kafir (Arabic): Apostate, Unbeliever.
17. Khamr (Arabic): Wine.
18. Khuda (Urdu): Lord, Allah.
19. Lakshman Rekha (Sanskrit): The bright-line rule.
20. Maghreb (Arabic): Northwest Africa.
21. Mashak (Arabic): Water bag made out of goatskin.
22. Mashrabiya (Arabic): Traditional architecture in the Islamic world.
23. Mashriq (Arabic): The eastern part of the Arabic world.
24. Mofata-al-dajaj (Arabic): Traditional dish of chicken with basmati rice.
25. Mulhid (Arabic): Atheist.
26. Nawab (Hindi/Urdu): A Mughal viceroy or an independent ruler in British India.
27. Padachon/Padachone (Malayalam): The Creator.
28. Poda Patti (Malayalam): Get lost, you scoundrel.
29. Porompokku (Malayalam): Unused government land near roads, railway tracks, etc.
30. Sagwan (Arabic): Teakwood.
31. Sjambok (Arabic): Heavy leather whip with sharp metal pieces.
32. Themmadi Kuzhi (Malayalam): Sinners' corner in a church cemetery.
33. Tu Kahan Hai (Hindi/Urdu): Where are you.
34. Umma (Malayalam): Mother.
35. Veshya (Malayalam/Sanskrit): Prostitute.
36. Yajif Jayidan (Arabic): A dry well.

Chapter One

THE SILENCE

There were heavy footsteps, like the swishing of the guillotine that severed pigs' heads in George Mooken's abattoir, and Thoma Kunj counted them, keeping his left ear close to the floor of the cell; a forewarning that the gallows were ready for him. His mother, Emily, had refused to abort him; nevertheless, twenty-four years later, a judge decided to hang him by the neck till he died. Thoma Kunj never knew the judge was his biological father.

He was thirty-five, healthy and sane.

The sounds were distinct, five persons, four well-built, wearing boots, and a tiny man, probably in sandals. Thoma Kunj waited for them for one year when the President rejected his final appeal. He slept in silence till three, and when he woke up, he tried to listen to the minutest sounds of the night. Typically, executions were early in the morning, around five. Every night from three to five-thirty, he expected the footsteps.

As the prison was on one hundred acres of land and considerably away from the main road, an eerie silence engulfed it like a harem in the middle of the Arabian desert. Mohammed Razak, a life-term convict, narrated to Thoma Kunj his experience at Unayzah in Qassim, where he spent his adolescence and youth and the diabolic silence in a harem. It was in a dates palm plantation owned by Muhammad Akeem and his son Adil, wherein they kept women from Malaysia, Pakistan, Lebanon, Iraq, Turkey, Azerbaijan and Egypt. Amira, about eleven years old, a Pakistani girl with greenish eyes and a cherubic face, loved talking in Urdu with Razak. Her grandparents' ancestors, Nawabs in Lucknow, fled to Islamabad during the partition of India, hiding gold sheets under their Gharara. She was probably the youngest among the concubines, an illegal migrant without a valid visa. But Akeem was happy to get her as he had many connections all over Arabia, and the agents contacted him whenever young girls were available. Once the courtesans crossed thirty-five to forty, Akeem sold them into the underworld, mainly in Riyadh.

Akeem called his mansion Mashrabiya and each doxy Bahiya, a gorgeous girl.

It was a Mashriq-style Mashrabiya of typical Islamic architecture, with an enclosed oriel window of carved woodwork and stained glasses. The Mashrabiya had three floors, and the women occupied the two upper floors. Razak's primary duty was serving food that he enjoyed thoroughly. He liked the smell and sounds of women and their colourful costumes.

Razak spent long hours with them playing cards. Singing was considered sinful or haram, but women from Egypt, Azerbaijan, and Malaysia sang folksongs by clapping each other's hands. Razak often joined them whenever Akeem was away. Their songs were mainly about love stories, separations, the longing to return to their birthplace, and meeting loved ones. They went deep into the heart of Razak and created feelings of sadness, sorrow, agony and separation. Razak sang for them Malayalam songs from Chemmeen and other movies.

The vast dates palm plantation, which he watched from the oriel windows, was planted by Akeem's father, who came from Yemen as a boy. The plantation was in an oasis wholly owned by him, about one hundred kilometres from Unayzah. Akeem was his only son among twelve daughters from three wives.

The harem women gossiped that Akeem's father enjoyed hunting and spent many days in the desert with friends and his son. In one such hunting expedition, Akeem assassinated his forty-eight-year-old father; a spear pierced his heart from behind while relishing roasted gazelle meat on charcoal. A formidable atlatl thrower, he could kill an Arabian tahr or an oryx with a single throw from about twenty metres. Akeem was only twenty-seven when he slayed his father as he wanted to take over his father's dates palm estate, the harem and the wealth he created.

Twice a week, Akeem dined with his mistresses, and they looked forward to celebrating by eating and drinking whatever they liked. Khamr, a wine brewed in the Mashrabiya, was taken with Mofatah al-dajaj, chicken pieces served over aromatic basmati rice cooked with cardamom, cinnamon, dried lemon, ginger and shaiba roots. On feast days, they cherished Jalamah, the meat of young lambs cooked with onion and a blend of spices, mainly black pepper. The most relished food by them was Gursan, thin bread with meat, vegetables, and arak, an alcohol distilled from fermented wheat, raisin and jaggery.

Akeem always expressed joy in meeting his lovers and loved their company. He presented expensive gifts to them and Razak whenever he returned from his foreign tours. Travelling to Europe and the Americas to export his best quality dates, he imported the latest machinery for his dates palm plantation, besides hickory, red oak and acacia wood for the shaft of spears. At least once in six months, he toured different parts of Arabia to buy girls and sell women.

At times, he was violent and forbidding, and most women hated him in their hearts. Mainly at night, when agents came to buy women who crossed forty, he whacked the ones who refused to go with a sjambok, a heavy leather whip, and the flogging continued for long hours, with screeching and shouting that disturbed Razak's sleep in a tiny room near the kitchen. As years passed, Akeem enticed new girls across the borders, and old ones disappeared. Amira appeared in the Mashrabiya only a few months before Razak reached there and was Akeem's favourite after weekly dinners.

Akeem had two wives, the free women, one from Yemen and the other from Iraq, and they lived in different twin palaces, built in the Maghreb style, adjacent to the harem. Adil was the son of the Yemeni wife, and he was not allowed to go to the harem.

Akeem had prohibited Razak from visiting the Maghreb.

Razak had left his family in Malabar when he was twelve years. An agent in Riyadh took him to Unayzah, and for the next nineteen years, he served in Akeem's seraglio without ever visiting his family in Malabar. Adil was only five years when Razak reached there, and they became friends, shared food, played two-men soccer in the courtyard of the Maghreb, learned Arabic, read the Quran, and prayed together. The silence within the Mashrabiya was scary, except for the shrieks of women in the middle of the night. Razak's story agonised Thoma Kunj, and he often experienced the fiendish silence and the sporadic shrieks within his stillness.

Adil cried loudly, watching Akeem castrating his friend Razak. When Razak was bedridden for two months because of the septic wounds, Adil cared for him. Once again, he yowled when circumcision was performed on him as Adil reached six years, thinking his father was castrating him and he would become like Razak. He felt thrilled to see he was still a male and started his sexual encounters with girls from Lebanon at fourteen. Soon, Akeem gave half of his estate to Adil, who established his harem in another corner of his estate.

When he went hunting, Akeem never took his son.

Akeem's women were kind to Razak. They presented him with expensive chocolates, good clothes, and perfumes, and when no one was around, they hugged and kissed him passionately and enticed him to play sex games they liked. Many nights, he slept with someone knowing well Akeem would decapitate him if caught. The concubines lured Razak, hiding him within their flowing abayas, and often overpowered him with sexual urges. Their supple body had a magnetism, an inexplicable vigour. The sex-starved courtesans craved caressing, warm togetherness with repeated orgasms. But they were many, and Razak fell flat in pleasing all of them.

Razak remembered Akeem searching for him with a scimitar the day he caught Razak sharing the bed with a courtesan from Egypt. Like a wild leopard in Ras Musandam whose cub was eaten by a striped hyena, Akeem was in a rage. Blood dripped from the blade that he held in his right hand.

Under his left arm was the Egyptian's severed head.

"Allah," Akeem roared.

There was absolute silence within the Mashrabiya.

"In your name, I will sacrifice the kafir, the Mulhid," Akeem's cry reverberated everywhere.

Mournful wailings of women filled the air of the Mashrabiya; they were lamenting the impending fate of Razak, who hid under the mattress covered in a pile of old clothes. For two days, he was there without food and water. The steel coil under the futon made deep cuts on his back.

On the third night, two women rescued him and fed him food and water. They cleaned his body and applied lotion on his back. He could see blood-soaked clothes in their hands. There was no leeway to escape from the Mashrabiya, and women opened the cover of a cellar, a rectangular catacomb, about eight feet in length and six feet in width, from the second floor to the ground without a door or window, about thirty feet in depth. It was built, touching walls on two sides. Akeem called it Yajif Jayidan, a dry well, a Jahannam, the hell for his concubines. Old clothes, discarded drivels, abayas, underclothes, and pads were stacked in the cellar. The women asked Razak to go deeper and hide in a safer depth, as they knew Akeem would come back with a spear to pierce his brain.

Razak went deeper, making his way through the rubbish. Breathing was strenuous, and the foul smell choked him, but it was more pleasing than the fear of death. Discarded pads with dried and fresh menstrual blood covered his face, and whenever he opened his mouth for a deep breath, it tasted bitter. He settled at a depth of about fifteen feet. Beyond that, he would be choked to death; visibility was poor. The pressure from overhead bunkums was too heavy, and it was difficult to lie down. He stood relatively straight, breathing heavily.

And Akeem came back on the fourth night. He had a spear, and a sudden silence spread in all the corners of the harem like the morning mist within the dates farm. The silence was heart-piercing. He poked inside the cellar from above with his spear for some time, but it could not penetrate deep into it as abayas, nighties, pyjamas, undies, and swobs blocked its path; pulling it back was stiff. There were no fresh blood drops and flesh on the spear's tip, so he went back cursing but promising to award the death penalty to the Kafir for Allah's glory.

The spear was a pole weapon, about seven feet in length, with a shaft made of hickory wood; the pointed head was steel. Akeem had a collection of more than one hundred lances with rods made from hickory, red oak, and acacia. Hickory and red oak were from California, and acacia from Western Australia, all Akeem personally imported. He hunted cape hares, sand cats, red foxes, caracals, gazelles, and oryxes in the desert with his trusted lieutenants for five to seven days once in six months. Except for spears and daggers, they used no other weapons. The expedition team consisted of about twenty people, only males, and they cooked and slept in the desert. They drank cans filled with arak and feasted on-skinned animals roasted whole over the sagwan wood fire.

On the fifth day, around noon, Razak heard a gentle voice; he could recognise it; it was Amira's. She was coming down, parting the garbage, and he heard her calling his name, "Razak, Razak, tu kahan hai?"

She had a bottle of water and some food. She cleaned Razak's face and lips with the dupatta draped around her neck. "Drink it," she said, giving him the bottle. Razak drank it slowly. The food was mutton biryani. She tore the meat into small pieces and fed him with her fingers. The little girl from Pakistan had grown into a beautiful woman but was condemned to be a sex slave in the netherworld of Arabia within a few years. From a harem, she would be transferred to a brothel.

Just as nursing a child, Amira took more than half an hour to finish feeding. Then she kissed the cheeks of Razak, pressed his face over her breast, and hugged him.

"Take me with you when you escape from here. I love to live with you anywhere in the world, please," Amira pleaded.

Razak looked at her, but he remained silent.

"This is the Jahannam described in the Quran; Akeem is Iblis," she continued after a pause.

"Yes, Amira," he replied.

"Razak, I don't believe in Khuda, who is nasty and brutish. As a male, he hates women; he is lustful and created a paradise with houris, young, full-breasted maidens, for the enjoyment of men. In Jannah, women are sex slaves. There were true stories of sex-starved illiterate thugs who captured women of all ages after war or night raids and married them forcefully in Arabian deserts. The marauders slashed the heads of their men on the battlefield. They believed if they died for Islam, they would get the houris, seventy-two of them in paradise. It was a great enticer," Amira said while hugging Razak.

"Women are concubines on earth and houris in heaven. Allah created women for men's pleasure," Amira stopped for a while when speaking.

"Razak, please take me; otherwise, I will end up in a whorehouse somewhere in Arabia," she said after a pause.

"Amira, I will, certainly," Razak made a promise. But she might not have heard him as his voice was too feeble.

While climbing, Amira looked at Razak.

"Kiss the sole of my right foot as a sign of trust. I have seen my father kissing the feet of his women in secret," Amira requested.

Razak kissed the sole of her right foot. It was soft and soaked in menstrual blood.

"Amira, we will go to Ponnani and live like the Nawab of Malabar," Razak promised.

Then Razak slept.

The following morning, he saw an old bundle of clothes near his left shoulder, and to get some more air to breathe, he pushed it away. The stench from the bale was unbearable; his fingers went into it when he touched it, and the clothes slipped out. Rotten human flesh covered his fingers, and an eyeball was in his palm, staring at him.

"Padachone," he cried.

It was the decomposing body of a newborn.

Razak vomited and tried to jump out, but his legs and hand got trapped. He heaved once again; some water and saliva came out.

Once more, he tried to part the old clothes and twaddle all around him, and his leg plunged into another putrid body, a baby thrown into the crypt immediately after its birth. He wanted to escape, jump out from the vault. Let Akeem cut his head. Razak fainted and lost consciousness.

When he opened his eyes, he thought he was in paradise surrounded by houris. It took a few seconds to realise they were the women of the harem who pulled him out of the cellar. He was nude, and they cleaned him with warm water, dried his body with Turkish towels, and covered him with fresh clothes.

"Razak, don't be afraid; he has gone to Riyad and shall be back only after seven days," Amira said.

He could not believe his ears. They were the most beautiful and consoling words he had ever heard, much more musical than the soliloquies he had when he ran away from his drunkard father at Tirur. His father, Bappa, had two wives and eight children. Razak was the eldest. Bappa had a teashop in Tirur fish market, and with his wives and children, he lived in an adobe shack close to the teashop. The money earned from the teashop was insufficient for the family, as he spent more than half the amount on alcohol daily.

Razak called his mother, umma, who went around selling fish. She carried the fish basket over her head and walked up to nearby villages; she cleaned the fish and cut it into pieces as homemakers asked. Pleased with her work, they gifted her old clothes, rice, coconut oil and spices at festivals like Onam, Vishu and Eid. But that was not sufficient; hunger lurked in the life of Razak, and only a few days a year, he ate a full meal with total satisfaction. He went to school to have the midday meal, a porridge of insipid taste.

Razak slept close to his umma and four other siblings on the floor. His second umma and her three children were in another corner. He could feel the starvation pangs of his siblings. Drunken squabbles of his Bappa with physical violence were typical, and often, he heard his mother's faint sobs.

Umma always smelled fish, and Razak loved that smell; he adored his mother. His only dream was to provide her with sufficient food and new clothes. Later, he dreamt of having a better house where umma could sleep on a cot and cover her body with a blanket to escape the cold during the monsoon. He fantasised about a bike to take his mother and siblings to the cinema once every month.

Friends told Razak stories of many young people who went to Saudi Arabia and the Gulf countries to make money. Those countries had enough gold; children played with gold, and even cars and houses were built. He knew many young people brought the shining metal to Malabar in small boats. But he did not realise it was smuggling, and if caught, he would be in prison for several years. Smuggling made many wealthy in Tirur, Ponnani, Ottapalam, Malappuram, and Kozhikode. They bought land, built shops, and started hotels, restaurants and hospitals. His friends told him all mansions around his mud house were constructed with money from gold from Saudi Arabia and Gulf counties.

Razak wanted to go to Arabia, bring back gold to feed umma, educate his siblings, build a house, buy a car, open a shop, and live happily ever after. He brooded over it for six months and discussed it with school friends. No one discouraged him. To get rich was his right, they said. They were also ready to go, and some had already gone. He noticed the number of students in the school diminished daily. Two of his close friends had left the previous week. When he reached the school, someone told him his class teacher had gone to UAE. The Arabian dream was spreading everywhere, and even children were restless.

One night, Razak ran away from home, not telling his mother. He felt sad leaving her, and he moaned alone. He knew he would come back soon with bags full of glittering metal. Many boats were going to different ports on the Arabian Peninsula, and he took one filled with young people who had been at sea for three days. An agent in the boat took Razak to Riyad with three other boys, all slightly older, and introduced him to another agent. Within three days, Razak was in the Mashrabiya of Akeem.

Razak slept for two days, surrounded by the women of the harem. The love they expressed for him was heavenly, like the houris of paradise, the reward for faithful Muslim believers in the afterlife, for pleasure, about whom he had read in the Arabic Quran.

Adil helped Razak escape from Arabia with a Mashak, a goatskin water bag filled with gold. He thought about his beloved Amira, the Pakistani whose greenish eyes he had kept within his eyes, and her appearance was in his heart. She had a beautiful soul filled with love; he wanted to take her with him and pleaded with Adil. But Adil disagreed, saying his father would slice the other women's throats if one were missing.

Razak was confident. Amira knew he could not have regular sex, so she accepted it, and after undergoing a hellish experience in the harem, she hated having sex. That would have solved many of his problems. He needed a companion, a woman who could love him, for whom he was ready to die. He wanted to share his life with Amira till his last breath. There was enough wealth to build a castle on the shore of the river Nila. For Razak, Amira would have been his best companion, the most trusted friend, his soul's soul, whose sole he had kissed. He longed for her presence, searched for her face, to be mystified with her lovely eyes, her soft cheeks, and her enchanting smile. Razak loved to share his dreams with her, past and future. He and she were beyond sex, the most depressing act on earth and in paradise. There were not interested in lovemaking anymore but in companionship, love, touch, and warm togetherness. Sometimes he thought he loved Amira more than his umma and felt sad about it, ashamed of the sin of loving a Pakistani woman more than his mother.

Razak remembered Amira coming down the Jahannam, feeding him biryani. Her soft, pretty fingers touched his lips. She had a gorgeous heart, a heart filled with love, more precious than the gold in his Mashak. He was ready to exchange all gold for her and her alone. From the beginning, he had loved her, never telling her.

He feared how she would react, as he was a castrated man, a rejected human, neither woman nor man. But with one word, she changed his world, rewrote history, and altered the plots of all epics ever written. She asked: "Razak, tu kahan hai?"

Amira was interested in his safety, and she existed for him. "I love you," she said. It sounded valuable, more precious than anything in the world. He, too, loved her with all his heart and soul. "I don't believe in Khuda, who is nasty and brutish," she said. Amira loved Razak, even in hell; she preferred a Jahannam with Razak to paradise without him. She could deny Allah for her beloved; the Almighty could not exist when Razak existed. Amira was so frightened about her future in a brothel, where she would become a sex slave for hundreds; in the Mashrabiya, she had to please only one man. She wanted to escape from the Mashrabiya to be with her beloved Razak, where no houris, no believers, and no Allah could reach.

Amira was thirty when Razak left the Mashrabiya. But he forgot to tell Amira he did not believe in Allah, who did not stop his castration. After the brutal removal of his testicles, Razak became an atheist. Only people like Akeem Allah existed, who were brutish and nasty.

Razak purchased one acre of land and built a villa at Ponnani, overlooking the Arabian Sea. He developed a shopping complex within the town near the main junction. Many girls were willing to marry him, and he chose one from Beypore, near Calicut and married her, hiding the truth that he could not have sex. He was thirty-two, and she was sixteen. After one year, Razak caught his wife with her paramour, and with a Malappuram hatchet, he slashed both heads. Akeem possessed him like Iblis.

There was a racking smile when Razak completed his sharing. He gazed at Thoma Kunj for a long time, not expecting a reaction but to verify whether his friend had understood the deeper meaning of silence. Thoma Kunj could observe a baffling ambience burdening Razak's emotions as his face crumbled and lips looped. Razak was a sad man in silence.

"If Akeem hadn't castrated me, I would have had a son your age. But you are my son, my only son. After the prison term, come and stay with me in Ponnani," Razak said to Thoma Kunj.

Thoma Kunj looked at him in disbelief. He loved a Pakistani woman in a harem, but after twenty years in prison, he adopted a man as his son, condemned to die from a noose, baptised Christian but an atheist. Razak had only one friend in prison, Thoma Kunj.

Thoma Kunj had met him eleven years ago while working on the prison farm. Razak was on the verge of completing his twenty-year prison term. He was fifty-three. Within six months of his release from the gaol, Thoma Kunj received a wedding invite from Razak, handed over by the jailor. It was the second year for Thoma Kunj. Razak had decided to marry a girl from Malappuram. He searched for a companion like Amira, who could love Razak, not obsessed with sex, but would share his silence.

The silence was golden. But the quietness of the hostel warden had an enigmatic echo with an outward tenderness, or she might have acted as affectionate. After two minutes of contemplative calmness, she told the court she had seen Thoma Kunj dropping the minor girl's body in a well adjacent to the hostel. The flashback she presented in a few words stunned those in the court and struck the judge like thunder. It shattered the confidence of Thoma Kunj as her evidence sealed his fate. It was around five in the evening, and she saw a tall figure, an unshaven face running through the hostel corridor, opening the door towards the well nearby the pump house and dropping the body in the well. She was sure that it was Thoma Kunj.

Thoma Kunj was in the hostel only once, at the insistence of George Mooken. It was a Sunday, and Mooken told him he had a call from the hostel warden about a leak in the pipeline water within the hostel. As it was a Sunday, the plumber of the hostel was out of the station and unavailable. The warden requested Mooken to send someone to repair the fault. As Thoma Kunj was handling the plumbing work in the piggery, Mooken insisted he goes to the hostel and does the repair, but Thoma Kunj was reluctant to go; besides, he had many things to do at home. Mooken once again called Thoma Kunj in the noon with the same request.

Thoma Kunj went to the hostel around three in the afternoon. He wanted to complete the work within two to three hours. But he never imagined it would change his life and land him on the gallows.

Thoma Kunj looked at the warden in disbelief from the defendant's box, but her appearance was tender, and the grey hair that fell on her forehead camouflaged her lie, her stubbornness. Her spectacles were round and thick; her face reflected the pain created by a murder in a government-run working women's hostel. She was the last witness. The judge had no uncertainty in believing the testimony of a fifty-five-year-old civil servant.

Nonetheless, Thoma Kunj never thought about the possibility that a judge could decide his destiny even before the hearing. At about forty-eight years old, the judge held a never revealed secret in his heart as he suffered from a profound silence of his creation from the day a college student told him she would not abort her baby. He was a young lawyer, and she visited his office to invite him to talk about law and literature at her college. She introduced him to her teachers and companions in apt words filled with encomiums. Her intelligence, leadership and ability to communicate fascinated him.

She admired his analytical prowess and expertise in law. His ability to convince his audience with succinct words and phrases was unique.

Their friendship grew, and they often met, travelled on the young lawyer's bike to different places, and spent nights in warm proximity.

His silence shattered into smithereens when he saw Thoma Kunj in the court. The judge read the defendant's name in silence: Thomas Emily Kurien. It surprised him; he looked at Thoma Kunj in disbelief. There was a reflection of his face on Thoma Kunj's appearance.

Stillness had a vibration; it was pregnant with a woman's sorrowful screams. The judge's silence for twenty-five years reverberated with those yells.

An elderly hostel warden's witness had a consequence as it led to a verdict sealing the fate of a twenty-four-year-old man.

"Hang him by his neck till he dies."

The verdict was short and precise.

Emily, Thoma Kunj's mother, suffered a silence different from Akeem's concubines' softness and was distanced from the silence of the ageing hostel warden. Emily's silence was heart-twisting; it penetrated the body of Thoma Kunj and permeated the entire house. Her hush was gentle, generous and loving. Until Thoma Kunj turned twelve, she was reluctant to share her childhood memories and college days; instead, she narrated stories from novels and epics. Thoma Kunj listened to her in reverence without interfering with her descriptions. But he sensed she kept an insightful calm even while telling stories.

Thoma Kunj carried her memory in unfathomable silence. In prison, he always remembered her. It was an unbreakable bond, and he grew with her silence. He meditated over her silence and transformed the cell with her lovely presence.

In the first few months in the cell, nights were long and terrifying, but he became familiar with the scary darkness that passed as they merged with daylights and lost their indifference. Slowly night-time became more pleasing, hopeful and tranquil. In the dark, he saw himself better and became more conscious of his inner vibrations and the vibes of the cell. The cell was like the Yajif Jayidan, wherein Razak had spent three days and nights immersed in twaddle and decaying human flesh. Never compassionate or curious but cautious and persistent, the cell protected him like a forensic doctor with a corpse. Within its windowless four walls, he could count his breathing, heartbeats, palpitations and the delicate laments of stray ants searching for food and their companions. The sounds coming from outside the cell had a unique stature and meaning. After midnight the approaching waders had a different purpose. They carried death in their mighty hands.

But there was a craving for death even before hitting the face of Appu. His lips flooded with blood, his teeth fell apart, and his nose crushed. It was a mighty hit. "Your mother is a veshya," he shouted, and all the students heard him. Ambika had a frightened look. But smashing Appu's nose had its reasons. How dare he call Mama a prostitute? It was a punishment, not a deterrent, not corrections, but revenge, like the Sakuni's in the Mahabharata.

The death wishes germinated when some students gossiped and teachers expressed unwanted sympathy. It was an intense desire to disappear from existence. Even at birth, a nascent longing to die existed. Mama used to say her baby repetitively struggled to place the bedclothes over his face with his tiny hands, choking his breathing. Mama was right; dying had a thrill; it fulfilled the yearning to live. Mama, Papa, Appu, the hostel warden, the judge, the jailors and the pigs in George Mooken's pigsty wriggled day after day to die, to experience the touch of death, warm and cold, soft and rough. Watching Mama's lifeless body hanging from the cross in front of the church instilled the rotten purpose of life, a plain and brutal truth, but it created lasting pricking. The finality of life was death, and all longing in life was longing for death. Mama made her noose from the husk of coconuts. After midnight she walked up to the church, and she knew the massive stone cross as, every Sunday, she had put money in the box kept by the cross. Mama never forgot to light a candle and pray, folding her hands in silence. She begged the Sacred Heart of Jesus, the Virgin Mary, and St Thomas the Apostle, who converted her ancestors when he landed on the Malabar coast in AD 52, to protect Thoma Kunj and Kurien. She threw the rope above the hands of the cross and tied it with a loop by herself, using a plastic stool. The coil would have intimidated but caressed her neck and strangulated her to death.

Eleven years in prison taught Thoma Kunj many lessons; he could distinguish even the slightest night noise. Death was silent; it never made a noise. The preparation for death created sounds and fury. The silence in prison was an expression of mourning and grief. There was a hidden dirge in silence, and one needed to be very attentive in listening to it. It was like enjoying funeral music; it was beautiful, serene and joyous. No one would have played it if it were cacophonous, not melodious, blissful. At Mama's funeral, there was no music. The vicar refused to bury her in the cemetery, saying she was sinful and hanged herself. There was wickedness and lust in his eyes. Years later, George Mooken said he paid a massive sum to the vicar to allow a sliver of mud to dig Mama's grave, but he did not disclose the amount. Mooken understood the death wish of Mama as she was bidding to live.

Mama tried to get the sweeper's job in the government-run school. The appointment order elevated her spirits, and her silence vanished quickly. Her English was excellent, as she could read and write it well. She studied in a public school in Kodaikanal, but Mama could not complete her college graduation and had no teacher's training to teach in an elementary school. During her second year in college, she became pregnant and, after delivery, left for Malabar with Kurien, but he was not Thoma Kunj's father. Emily had told Papa even before the marriage about her relationship with a lawyer who ditched her. Papa's decision to marry Mama was not out of sympathy but love. Kurien worked in George Mooken's piggery, and Emily became a sweeper in a government school. Even the school's headmaster often sought her help to draft letters and circulars in English.

When Thoma Kunj was twelve, Emily shared her story with him; she thought her son should know it, and she was not ashamed. Thoma Kunj accepted her biography and held his head high.

The parish priest demanded a considerable sum, a bribe for the sweeper's job in the parish school, even though the government paid the salary in the church-run school.

To bury her in the church cemetery, the vicar accepted a sum.

Papa helped Mooken start his piggery, as he had had training in a veterinary college for one year and learned new techniques in hog breeding. He was the first full-time worker with Mooken and later trained fifteen workers and became the supervisor within ten years. They went to swine farms in Idukki, Wayanad and Coorg to buy truckloads of piglings. The pigpen flourished; Mooken exported pork to many restaurants and hotels all over India. He acquired lands and goods, cars and trucks, gifted fifty cents of land to Papa and helped him construct a house with three rooms, a kitchen and toilets. But before plastering it, Papa died. The Karnataka police beat him for no reason. For them, the truck had no valid pollution under control certificate, as it had expired two weeks before. Mooken might have forgotten to get the certificate, even though it was not a crime inviting capital punishment.

Often Karnataka police awarded harsh penalties to truck drivers from across its borders on flimsy grounds.

They demanded a bribe of two thousand rupees, and Papa refused to pay. Mooken would have paid the amount because he induced bureaucrats and the parish priest for various benefits, as without paying bribes, it was impossible to start a business. Papa wanted to save his employer's money, which led to his ruthless end. He was a small man; his fragile body could not resist the sadistic assault of the police, and he died there with severe injuries. He vomited blood. Some policemen were horrid and ruthless, and many behaved inhumanly to earn money. For them, Papa needed to pay the penalty for refusing to pay an inducement, which they considered their right. All death penalties were a violation of rights, factual or imagined. But some who received the death penalty were innocents. People were worried only about the victim, rarely concerned about the convict, among whom many had no hand in the crime. Society seldom cared about the innocence of a voiceless accused man. Someone must die and pay the ultimate price; after his death on the gallows or at the hands of the police, none bothered to verify whether the person who lost his life was innocent. Mama wept seeing Papa's broken arms and legs but could not imagine his shattered liver, punctured lungs, heart and pancreas.

The Karnataka police fabricated a story of a mad elephant crushing Papa's body. The enraged animal could not be caged. It just wandered into the mind of the police and those who heard about the story. Even after Papa's death, Mama weaved hope for life.

Hope and despair went hand in hand, and it wasn't easy to distinguish the occasions when they separated. When the judge pronounced the verdict, there was despair and anticipation, the anguish of losing a way of life, and eagerness to see the new. Even when he lost his final appeal, there was gloom and optimism-sadness at losing the cell but the anticipation of seeing the scaffolds. While standing on the gallows, there would be desolation and confidence. Death would be the absolute joy; the noose would tighten, and the body dangled in the air; it would challenge criminal law, the prison personnel, and Padachon. As Amira challenged Allah, Emily dared her crucified saviour; she could overcome death when others would shiver at its very thought.

Thoma Kunj kept his left ear close to the floor as the right one had partly lost its hearing ability in the police station when law-keepers assaulted him in custody.

Thoma Kunj heard the thud of metal keys unlocking the locks. The cell had double locks, two massive padlocks built in the prison's forge where he had worked for six years. He was in carpentry for two years and another two on the farm. After rejecting his final appeal, he was kept in a cell with double locks to close the escape routes. For one year, he had been waiting for the execution. Every morning there was anticipation for the footsteps and the boots' sound. Three to five-thirty in the morning was the most agonising time for fulfilling life; as Mama said: "This misery is the meaning of life, but there is a satisfaction in it." The waiting gave him hope and eagerness to listen to the solemn footsteps and the waders' heavy sound.

Walking along with the superintendent, two jailors, a guard, and a doctor had majesty. The hands would be tied from behind. It was a parade like that in the Janpath on Republic Day. As a member of the Boys Scouts, Thoma Kunj once participated in it. He was in the eighth class and was the only student selected from his school. The only difference was that marching to the gallows had no band, music or horses or did not require previous training. Thoma Kunj had three month's training for the Republic Day parade, two months in the district headquarters, and one month in New Delhi. Emily was alive then; she had watched the entire programme on TV. After the parade, he returned home with many gifts for his mother, Parvathy, George Mooken, teachers, and friends. There was a replica of the Red Fort for Ambika. Emily hugged him as she felt proud of him. The whole school celebrated it; he was a hero. But the parade with prison officers ended on the gallows. Usually, hangings took place early in the morning, around five. There were two nooses on the same gibbets, so two prisoners could be hanged simultaneously.

While pronouncing the death sentence, the judge said hanging was a painless punishment and best suited to Indian culture, even though it was introduced by the British. He was speaking as though he had experienced it. He might have undergone it in his mind a thousand times. Before the British Raj, the Mughals had a variety of methods to execute a convict, including crushing a prisoner's head with an elephant or cutting off his head with a sword, like a bunch of illiterate rogues conducting a night raid in the Arabian oasis populated by the Jews, for the pleasures with seventy-two houris in their afterlife.

The judge was a middle-aged man. Thoma Kunj would look like the judge when he touched his age. He had a slight grey beard, and Thoma Kunj had a dark one, as he could not shave his stubble when in the cell. After going through the case file and reading his name, the judge looked at him with curiosity. Thoma Kunj was the accused; the judge sent him to prison till the final hearing. The judge was a free man, and Thoma Kunj became an undertrial.

When convicted, Thoma Kunj worked in the furnace and was the best ironsmith. The jailor often said his craft was superb, like the Germans. Before taking charge of the prison furnace, the jailor had one year of training in a smithy in Völklingen. Thoma Kunj liked the heat and sound of the forge and the final products he shaped. He moulded the locks that locked him, and he was aware of it. "You mould your future, lock your life with it and throw the keys in a deep gorge," Mama said while cooking; she was speaking about the futility of life when left alone, friendless, voiceless. Thoma Kunj remembered her words when he was in the kiln, but he was pleased to shape the locks. Within the cell, he was safe; he knew it. The danger was outside the cell, the punishment room, the batons, the chain, and finally, the gibbets. "One chooses his destiny," was the opinion of the jailor. He believed in Karma.

The jailor of the smithy believed humans are created free, and everyone possesses free will; they do what they like. Once they broke the law, they would be responsible for their actions and deserved punishment. But he was different from other jailors, as he never whipped convicts and did not even abuse them. His hands were not dirty with prison money and property. In contrast, the superintendent and other officers freely indulged in amassing wealth, which made the jailor of the smithy a misfit in prison. Thoma Kunj respected him but adjudged his philosophy on crime to be naïve.

The jailor was a believer and offered prayers every day. He had built a tiny place of worship in his house, adjacent to the dining hall, where he and his wife offered prayers to Ganesh, the elephant god, with flowers, burning oil lamps, and incense. Reciting the Vakratunda Ganesh Mantra, he spent at least half an hour before the idol.

Humans were free only in a limited sense, and their past, present and future were determined, with no escape. But everyone possessed the ability to endure adversities and woe, to win as humans could shape their immediate surroundings. After three days of an epic battle, a lonely old angler caught a giant marlin much bigger than his boat in the middle of the sea. He reeled the marlin in, lashed it, tied it by his catamaran's side, and rowed towards the coast. Sharks attacked the fish, and the fisherman fought against them relentlessly. Reaching the shore, the piscator found the extended skeleton of the fish he caught, and people crowded to watch it. That night, he slept dreaming of lions. Mama narrated the story; Thoma Kunj could not grasp the whole meaning. But he learned humans were there to win.

Thoma Kunj disliked piety and hated God. The day his mother hanged herself from the cross in front of the church, he burned images of the sacred heart of Jesus, the Virgin Mary and saints from the walls of his house. Making a bundle of the ashes in a plastic bag, he threw it in a pit where George Mooken collected pigs' urine to produce cooking gas. Thoma Kunj stopped going to church after the burial of his mother. He swore he would never enter a church or worship a cruel and narcissistic God. Razak's story confirmed that Padachon was evil, as humans could not think about an all-powerful, eternal entity that was not wicked.

At least once every month, when the sun dipped in the sea and darkness engulfed the country or early in the morning when no one was around, he visited Emily's grave and shared his stories with his Mama.

The sympathy Thoma Kunj hated as he knew compassion was a tool to create piousness and obedience. He attended church every Sunday and on feast days with his mother to worship when the vicar said prayers in Malayalam mingled with Aramaic-Syriac. Thoma Kunj had read the Bible from the first word to the last, but even as a child, he disliked the God of Israel, who was cruel and bloodthirsty and killed children and women. Emily told him not to read the Old Testament but encouraged him to learn from the New Testament, where Jesus was the main character. But he refused to believe the miracles he performed, especially converting water into wine at Cana and raising Lazarus from the dead. Thoma Kunj laughed at the virgin birth.

After Emily's death, it was too late for him to realise that the Bible stories were myths like the Iliad and Odyssey, Mahabharata and Ramayana or the magic of the Merciful of the Arabian desert. Thoma Kunj felt sympathy for the God of Moses and Abraham when he became a man.

The God of the Bible was not silent; he was a roaring entity like Amira's. He created noise, hatred, emotional upheavals, revenge, lust, and Akeem's sword.

When Akeem beheaded the Egyptian woman, the Merciful was quiet. He kept a profound calm when newborns were thrown into Mashrabiya's hell in small cloth bundles, and Razak cried Padachone after his fingers pierced a decaying body. The Almighty kept quiet when Akeem created his harem with virgins from Malaysia to Egypt and Azerbaijan to Pakistan.

In Thoma Kunj's life, too, God was silent. His silence was heart-piercing when Papa was beaten to death by the Karnataka police on his way from Virajpet to Koottupuzha. God was silent when the vicar demanded a bribe to appoint Emily to the parish school as a sweeper, for which the government paid the salary. He kept a profound silence when the vicar demanded money to bury Mama's body in the parish cemetery.

The silence was internal; it had an endless universe, and one needed to die to understand it truly. It had no boundaries as no one could measure, share or hawser it. The stillness never achieved its fullness, exceeded its worth of not wanting anything, bursting with the freedom to have imagination, reflection and meditation in a vacuum. Cyclically lethargic, the silence was the most powerful being in human existence, ever pervading, constantly permeating, but putrid in appearance. In essence, it contradicted itself to grow in magnitude and stature, questioning its presence in void, the silence opposed definitions. It could hug you with everlasting empathy and stupefying expectations, a tentacle hard to escape. The quietness was different to different people; worthless, unauthenticated, self-destructive, alluring, enticing and ever enchanting. Thoma Kunj entered the stillness in a hush but never returned.

But the silence was no solution to evil.

Thoma Kunj was ready to penetrate his calmness, sleeping within his existence. It was frustrating as he repeatedly tried to touch the core of his being, emotions, and breathing to experience the profound longing to extinguish himself. Seeking to go beyond and share its heartbeats and consciousness with the self in him, he dived into the depths of his soul. The emptiness that engulfed him was full of mournful mists about his Mama and Papa that narrated stories of sorrow and anguish.

But the death wish was still in his silence, jumping over the rubrics of his beliefs to reach his parents, like Razak's quest to get Amira.

For ten years, he lived within the four walls of the prison as a convict, waiting for the result of his final appeal and, in the eleventh, expecting the superintendent, jailors, guards and the doctor to lead him to the gallows. For their footsteps, he waited from three to five-thirty in the morning, every day, every hour, every minute and every second.

And finally, they arrived.

He heard the sound of the key against the padlock which he had designed in the prison furnace. They locked him inside with the same padlock. When working in the furnace, Thoma Kunj knew he was making his lock to lock his cell.

His cell had only a dim lightbulb; its switch was outside.

The dim light had its silence.

During the night, there was light only from seven to eight. It was the light created by someone. In the last stage of his life, he discarded the self and existed beyond his existence. It was a contradiction but a reality for Thoma Kunj.

"You won't cry for life, you don't crave pleasures, you don't think of a future, and you forget the past," Thoma Kunj instructed himself.

"When you lose yourself, you don't see the noose, you don't touch its knot against your throat, and you don't see the scaffolds," he assured himself.

Razak could not overcome his frustration and re-lived his castration. Akeem gelded him only once, but Razak sterilised himself every minute of his life. Amira could go beyond frustration as she understood its insignificance and diminishing returns. She built a world with her love for Razak, a vision of togetherness, sharing and warmth. She was ready to travel with him, hug him with passion without exploiting his limitations, to relive his love for his umma. Amira became Razak, but he could not reciprocate it with his life. He was ready to leave her in hell, an earthly paradise, with earthly houris for Akeem. Amira had a love that broke all barriers of silence and pierced beyond where a spear could reach.

Amira descended into hell, and she dared to do it. She searched for Razak, and meeting him alive gave her happiness. Amira overcame death. For Emily and Amira, the silence was the existence of life without constraints, as it was a life without fear. Amira had no fear of going to hell and feeding Razak; Emily was intrepid in protecting the unborn against its biological father's wishes. She travelled beyond time, outside dread and hatred. Emily and Amira's silence transmitted an image of infinite space and eternal love. Mama gave up her silence to enjoy her freedom, as she could not suffer the calumny, the disgrace, the lie of a priest.

The judge's silence was predetermined as he believed in the devil's existence but forgot about his behaviour. When he was a lawyer, he insisted a young woman abort. The woman refused, and he kept a grudge in his heart when a judge sent her son to the gallows. He decided on the case even before the hearing. He had already sentenced Thoma Kunj while in his mother's womb. The judge brooded over the guilt he had as a lawyer, rejecting a woman he promised to provide togetherness, companionship and happiness. He carried it for many years; even though it was a rare coincidence, he celebrated it. He presented Thoma Kunj with the noose.

The silence created shadows and Thoma Kunj fought against the shades within his cell.

Suddenly the door of the cell opened and was kept ajar. The Superintendent, followed by two jailors, a guard, and a doctor, entered. There was a smell of death as the officers and the guards stood straight in uniform. The doctor was in mufti.

The guard tied the hands of Thoma Kunj from behind with irons and locked it. He handed over the key to the Superintendent.

The doctor took his pulse rate and heartbeats and diagnosed the general conditions of Thoma Kunj. Within two minutes, the investigation was over. Then he took the medical logbook and wrote the convict's name, age, health condition, date and time. In the next paragraph, he wrote:

"Thomas Kunj, aged 35, is fit to be hanged." He wrote his name and signed with the date and time.

The doctor gave the logbook to the superintendent. He read the details written by the doctor and wrote his name, and signed with the date and time.

He also wrote the names of the jailors and the guard and asked them to sign against their names with the date and time, and they did as he ordered.

"It is finished," said the superintendent.

The jailors came forward and stood on both sides of Thoma Kunj; the guard stood behind him. Then the Superintendent turned towards the door; the doctor stood behind him, and Thoma Kunj was behind the doctor. The Superintendent moved forward; it was the first step to the gallows. The judge had made the decision eleven years ago.

Thoma Kunj was silent. He was meditating on the noose.

Chapter Two

THE CELL

There were five free men and one convict in the cell, the prisoner condemned to be hanged by the neck till death. The cell was a windowless dungeon eight feet by eight feet, too small to accommodate all of them. The ventilation touching the roof above twelve feet for fresh air was not visible from the ground because of the thickness of the wall. The walls of the cell were built with granite boulders and cement. There were about twenty such cells in prison, situated in the district headquarters, a large town in Malabar on the seacoast.

Thoma Kunj's village, Ayyankunnu, was about fifty-five kilometres from the prison on the state highway leading to Mysore through Koottupuzha. There was a river flowing from Coorg, Kodagu in the local language, on his village's northern and western borders, touching a vibrant town called Iritty. The river emptied itself into the Arabian Sea near Valapattanam, a few kilometres north of the prison.

As swimming was his hobby during adolescence, Thama Kunj had crossed the river on many occasions, even during monsoons. Other boys were afraid or not interested in jumping in the water when the river was swollen, and the currents were deadly. When he was fifteen, Thoma Kunj got hold of a large wooden log about six metres in length, swept away in the water from the forest, and pulled it towards the bank, a herculean task to do alone, and pushed it in a safe place. On many occasions, such floating timbers hit the pillars of the Iritty iron bridge and damaged its columns or created an artificial dam that blocked water flow.

The next day, a constable went to his house and asked Thoma Kunj to meet the police inspector in his office. On reaching the police station, the officer was rude and accused Thoma Kunj of stealing the property of the forest department. Thoma Kunj told him he had no intention of stealing it; he wanted to save it for the forest department and keep the wooden log on the riverbank. Besides, he was trying to protect the bridge's columns from severe damage. The police officer was not ready to accept his reasoning, and Thoma Kunj had to visit the police station half a dozen times to convince the officer of his innocence. Often, the police played such games to extract money from innocent villagers. That was his first encounter with the police.

Since adolescence, he had been well aware that his father was beaten to death by the Karnataka police. The Kerala police were equally violent and cruel.

All the higher officers in the prison department were from the police. But those below the superintendent were from the prison system, specially trained officers handling convicts who suffered from multiple social and psychological problems. Some jailors had received training in management, social work, clinical psychology and counselling. Those trained officers behaved much more gently with the prisoners. The jailor of the smithy had undergone training in Germany.

Before rejecting his final appeal, Thoma Kunj worked in the forge and slept in the main dormitory that accommodated about fifty convicts. There were five such dorms, and they were comparatively more liveable than the cell.

A toilet was in one corner of his cell; running water was available only for one hour each morning and evening. A plastic mug was there for bathing, cleaning and drinking water, and Thoma Kunj slept on a mat spread on the floor; there was no pillow or a cot. The rug woven with dried leaves of screw pine plants looked rough, and he had seen such plants near streams and water bodies in Malabar. He had also seen women cutting the leaves of the screw pine plants, drying them in the sun and weaving mats. Various rugs were for infants, children and adults; some were colourful with rounded borders.

Thoma Kunj, Emily and Kurien slept on mats with a pillow on the floor in his childhood. He remembered his mother coming to his small room, talking to him, and covering his body with a light blanket every day just before he slept. He always waited for a parting kiss; it was sweet and soft. Before going back, she caressed his forehead, saying:

"Sleep tight, sleep well, my Kunj mon." She, at all times, called him Kunj mon. Mon in Malayalam means "beloved son".

"Love you, Mama," Thoma Kunj reciprocated her love and kissed her cheeks.

When he was eight years old, he slept on a cot for the first time. It was made out of teak wood. The lumber was donated by George Mooken, who had a score of gigantic teakwood trees on his farm. Thoma Kunj watched with wonder two labourers slicing the wood using a crosscut saw. The saw was designed to cut wooden logs across the wood grain. The workers called the saw Arakkawal, but George Mooken called it the thwart saw. The cutting edge of each tooth angled in an alternating pattern on the saw, which helped each tooth slice wood, similar to a knife edge. Thoma Kunj liked how labourers worked with the cross saw and wanted to join them. Gathering courage, he expressed his desire, but they frowned at him and reminded him to concentrate on his studies, to his disappointment.

Kurien called two carpenters to work from home, and they worked for ten days to make two cots. Thoma Kunj enjoyed watching the carpenters using their tools, especially hammers, tape measures, squares, marking pencils, screwdrivers, chisels, circular saws, and power drills. After two days, he told the head *mistri* he wanted to become a carpenter. The *mistri* laughed loudly, saying he should become an engineer instead. But Thoma Kunj insisted on being a carpenter and requested them to take him in their team. The other carpenter listening to him intently, told Thoma Kunj he could work with him for five minutes, and if he adored the carpenter's work, he would welcome him as his assistant, giving him a tape measure and marking pencil. Thoma Kunj was delighted to work as a carpenter for at least five minutes. He felt elated as he prized working with his hands.

Thoma Kunj treasured the fresh smell of teak, and the cots appeared to be fantastic. Mama purchased two cotton mattresses with pillows. The mattress rested on the cot's slat, and the bolster was placed over it. The bed and padding were lovely; lying on them was soothing. For the first time, Thoma Kunj slept on a cot. He folded the mat and kept it in his room as a memento, as sleeping on it helped develop solid muscles and facilitated regulating his body as per the floor's roughness, an unwanted fine-tuning to his future prison life.

The convicts slept on separate mats sans pillows. In prison, a pad was a luxury, and it was forbidden. A coarse cotton bed cover made in prison was given to cover the body to protect it from cold and mosquitoes. But in the cell, there was only a mat, no pillow, and no sheets to cover the body. During the monsoon, the cold was unbearable.

There was no chair or cot within the cell, so sitting on the ground for long hours was tedious and backbreaking. Often, Thoma Kunj remembered the rocking chair at home. Kurien had purchased a rocking chair made of rosewood within one year of getting the cot. The wood of the rocking chair was a deep reddish-brown with attractive markings of dark streaks and interlinked grains. It was a fabulous experience to sit on the rocking chair for hours together, and he sat on it every day whenever he had free time. On the last day at home, he was rocking on the chair and saw the police officers coming. He had just returned from the working women's hostel.

Generally, Thoma Kunj had much work in the piggery on all days except Sundays. That Sunday, he went to the women's hostel to repair the faulty pipeline connecting the overhead water tank. It was a minor repair, and no immediate restoration was required. The warden could have waited for one more day, even a week. Calling him on a Sunday was unnecessary; she could have asked the plumber to do the work. The plumber of the hostel might have seen the water leakage; he might have left it for another day. Thoma Kunj doubted the intentions of the hostel warden, as it was unnecessary to call an unknown person to a women's hostel on a Sunday to do the work. He had to drive his bike for twenty minutes to reach the hostel. He accepted the job only because George Mooken insisted. The warden knew George Mooken as he supplied milk, meat and eggs to the hostel.

Thoma Kunj prepared a cup of tea and sipped it while rocking. At nightfall, he saw three people approaching, and when their faces were visible, he realised they were policemen in mufti, an inspector and two constables. It was the last time he sat on his favourite rocking chair.

The absence of a chair or cot initially created uneasiness, as there was no room to walk in the cell. But Thoma Kunj exercised every morning and evening for an hour to escape the weakening of the muscles, body aches, palpitations, and sheer boredom.

Thoma Kunj never knew why the square cells were for the condemned prisoners. Once in a barrack, he had overheard from a jailor that it was a British custom to have square cells for the condemned prisoners as there were fewer suicide rates in such cells. One reason was that there was limited space for walking and jumping in a square. Besides, it was more soothing to the mind than any other shape. Prisoners in a circle or an oval-shaped cell developed mental tensions and hallucinations much faster than convicts in a square enclosure. The British had their hypotheses; some were still hunches, not verified theories. When they built a gaol in Malabar in 1869, they tried to apply the experiences they gathered from other prisons in British India, especially from Madras.

The cell floor was paved with massive granite sheets from the colossal granite hills on the Western Ghats. George Mooken's house was tiled with polished granite sheets from Mysore and rough granite on the courtyard from Coorg. Papa had bought semi-polished granite from Madikeri.

British criminal law required that the floor be harsh in the prison cell, like a convict's life. Based on the moral cogitations of Jeremy Bentham, the rule book suggested extreme punishments for the convicts. For the rationalists, crime was a free-will decision, as all humans were created with free will, and individuals acted in ways that maximised pleasure and minimised pain. The only remedy to eliminate crime was the deterrent punishment. Still, the application of revenge was explicit in Her Majesty's Criminal Justice System adopted from Hammurabi in Mesopotamia, akin to an "eye for an eye and a tooth for a tooth." Only two categories of prison personnel were needed initially: the keeper of the gaol and the hangman.

Thoma Kunj had never heard about either Hammurabi or Bentham, yet, he suffered enormously because of their vengeful deterrent and hedonistic criminal justice legal system. A prisoner never knew his suffering was due to the crazy rancorous beliefs of a Mesopotamian monarch and an English utilitarian. Her majesty's criminal justice administration gifted suffering and misery to millions of prisoners as it was based on Hammurabi's dictums. Even though the British were hesitant to accept the Mesopotamian monarch openly, they proudly embraced the utilitarian notions of Bentham, the moralist, whose obscurantism and ignorance about social, psychological, and biological antecedents of crime smarted Thoma Kunj in a remote corner of Malabar as an independent India slavishly encompassed the irrational idiosyncrasies of her masters of yesteryears.

Thoma Kunj did not understand why he was suffering, which resulted from a proposal called the pleasure-pain principle, and punishment consisted of inflicting pain on the offender. He never intentionally broke the law to experience pleasure; he was innocent. A preacher who lived two and half centuries ago in England decided his fate. A judge, a brilliant wordsmith, in Thalassery sentenced him to die on the gallows, accepting the teachings of Bentham he learnt by heart in a nondescript law college. He, too, was an admirer of the deterrent principle, forgetting his escapades in pleasures. The judge could not think beyond hedonism; his mind was framed accordingly. The law books authorised him to punish persons who caused pain to others, and the judge was part of a system established by the British devoid of knowledge of human behaviour. The judge punished Thoma Kunj not for his guilt but for being a young lawyer's unwanted child. The judge's mind was predetermined by a woman who had refused to abort her baby, and Thoma Kunj was the product of that guilt. The judge forgot about the pleasures he derived as a young lawyer in distant Kochi, causing pain to that woman and her child.

The cell had an opening with a cement frame which had a width of two feet, and the door was fitted from the outside with no door handle from the inside; it could not be opened from the inside.

In the initial days in the cell, Thoma Kunj drew pictures of his Mama on the cell wall with his imagination. At first, there was only one image, but gradually he created more of them, and within a week, he filled the four walls with his Mama's smiling face. The images were of actions in the second week: Mama cooking, working, sweeping, talking, eating, or washing clothes. Then he added his Papa's pictures. He coloured the images of Mama and Papa, turning them into a movie with diverse titles, love stories, action movies, thrillers, crime detectives, and historical films. Mama played the queens of yonder years with a crown and flowing royal gowns, and Papa was always there by her side. They never played the villain but the heroine and hero. Directing, producing, editing, releasing, and watching his movies was time-consuming; weeks and months passed, and Thoma Kunj worked tirelessly and enjoyed his creations.

He divided the walls into four sections and started painting sceneries: hills, rivers, valleys, forests, grasslands, animals, birds, farmlands, fruit trees such as coconuts, jackfruits, mangoes, banana trees, coffee bushes with berries, and pineapples. He watched them with happiness and walked around them for days and weeks. He hugged his trees, talked to them endlessly, and swore he wouldn't cut them. The trees were lively, charming and strong and stood on the hillside, the riverbank, valleys and borders of the grasslands. For Thoma Kunj, trees were the most beautiful creation on Earth, and he could not imagine an Earth without trees. In his world of imagination, there were hundreds of varieties of trees, columnar trees, open-head trees, weeping trees, drooping trees, fastigiate trees, vase-shaped trees, and horizontal trees. There were also running, jumping, sleeping, laughing, dancing, and singing trees. All were unique, beautiful and lovely. All the varieties had exceptional flowers, fruits and seeds.

He found they could communicate with each other and the universe and express their joy, worry, and sorrow with amazement. The inimitable leaves of trees astounded him; some were too small as the head of a needle, some bigger than an elephant's ears,

When the monsoon came, the trees danced in the rain; in winter, they slept, covering their body under thick blankets; in summer, new leaves and flowers appeared with expectations, fruits ripened, and they invited animals and birds to have a banquet under their shades and on the branches. Trees were the most selfless beings on the planet, and they gifted their total wealth, including themselves, to others.

Imitating his Papa, when he was four years old, Thoma Kunj planted a couple of jackfruit and mango seeds on the corners of their land. Within four years, flowers appeared, and there was an abundance of luscious jackfruits and mangoes. He danced joyfully and presented a jackfruit and basketful of mangoes to Parvathy, George Mooken's wife. She hugged Thoma Kunj affectionately and offered him a woollen jacket she had brought from Bangalore. After tasting the ripened jackfruits and mangoes, George Mooken visited Thoma Kunj, and with him and Kurien, he went to see the jackfruit and mango trees, touched them, and expressed his joy. George Mooken and Parvathy were lovers of trees, and they planted hundreds of varieties of trees on their farm, brought from different countries. That day, George Mooken presented Thoma Kunj with a majestic study table and a chair; the tabletop was from a single piece of mahogany; the sidebars were teak, and the drawers and legs were of rosewood; the combination looked terrific. The chair was rosewood, and Thoma Kunj treasured both.

Thoma Kunj created farmlands on another wall; the tiny adobe houses, children playing, and women and men working in the paddy fields looked surreal yet peaceful. There were schools, playgrounds, and classrooms with students and teachers. In his world of imagination, the planet was green and beautiful. There was no pain, suffering or illness. His Mama and Papa were there constantly.

He painted the house of George Mooken and Parvathy, a woman who left her father and their prosperous coffee plantation in Coorg to marry a man she loved. In August 1972, a twenty-four-year-old Parvathy ran away with twenty-five-year-old Mooken, who waited for her under the coffee bushes for days together. George Mooken carried her on his shoulders while crossing the Western Ghats from Deva Moily's mansion to his small house in Ayyankunnu. He walked from three in the morning to eight at night through the coffee plantation on the eastern slopes of the Sahyadri, the thick rain forest with animals roaming majestically, and the rubber and cashew tree plantation on the western slope of the mountain. Parvathy had just completed her MBA in plantation management.

Parvathy's father owned two hundred acres of a coffee estate with tall trees covered with black pepper vines.

Deva Moily, her father, was one of the wealthiest persons in Coorg; his only son, a colonel in the army, died in the 1965 India-Pakistan War.

George Mooken graduated in agriculture and animal husbandry from a university in Pant Nagar. He had taken fifty acres of land on lease for ginger cultivation in Coorg and worked with the labourers daily. The ginger cultivation was near Parvathy's coffee estate. On her visit to the nearby fields, Parvathy saw a new farmer working with the farm labourers; she stopped her car, went to the area and initiated a discussion with George Mooken. It was an enlightening talk, and Parvathy realised the farmer was an educated man full of dynamic, practical ideas on farming and animal husbandry. Their conversation happened daily, and they talked about everything under the sun, including epics, novels, short stories, and human psychology. Parvathy's admiration for her farmer friend had no boundaries. The respect turned into love, and George Mooken reciprocated with eagerness and openness. He accompanied her to other coffee estates within Coorg, and they returned the same evening. Those outings were intense and revealing; they learned about each other, their personalities, abilities, capacities, and drawbacks. They shared ideas, and hypotheses and built a world of fervent hope and desires around them.

Parvathy and George Mooken fell in love and decided to spend the rest of their life together. Convincing her father was impossible as he had many plans for his daughter. Alarmed and hurt by his daughter's decision,

Deva Moily was in a rage for many days and became adamant like the granite boulders over the Brahmagiri peak. Parvathy decided to run away with George Mooken without informing Deva Moily.

Thoma Kunj looked at his painting of George Mooken and Parvathy on the wall and admired their tenacity in achieving their goal of being with each other till death. Thoma Kunj also felt such love towards Ambika; he thought she kept her passion for him burning for a long time. It started when they were in the eighth grade. But it was unexpressed for many months, and when she talked about it, they celebrated it, not knowing it would be short-lived.

Some days, Thoma Kunj sat idly, not doing anything, and there was nothing to do. His active mind rested. He thought about his eleven years in prison, working on the prison farm where he met Razak. Then he was in carpentry, where he learned various work and loved the sounds of tools and aromas of wood. Each wood had a different fragrance, and the most pleasing smell was that of teak, rosewood and jackfruit trees. Teak was water and white ant-resistant with a dense structure yet lightweight. Most furniture was built with teak, and it was in high demand. Rosewood was rarely available and known as the king of trees with a brownish or reddish hue and darker veining. All the cabinets and wall cupboards in George Mooken's house were rosewood, as rosewood did not require polishing due to its elegant, distinguished and magnificent grains. Rosewood lasted for hundreds of years. The jackfruit tree and wild jack called Anjili were graceful and splendid. Sheesham wood was rare but elegant looking.

Thoma Kunj thought of opening a carpentry shop if his appeal against the death penalty was successful. After serving a life term, he would return to his village; his carpentry would attract several customers as he had learned the latest techniques and methods in woodworking. He would inform Razak they would meet at Ayyankunnu or Ponnani to celebrate and reminiscence their victory over their prison life.

The introduction of treatment, corrections, skill development, employment, counselling, social work, and rehabilitation of prisoners resulted from the French Renaissance. Research findings in sociology, psychology, human behaviour, counselling and social work influenced gaol officers to be enlightened and work for prisoners' welfare. But no social worker, counsellor, or human rights activist was there to think about Thoma Kunj, as he had no parents, relatives, or friends and was not related to politicians. He was voiceless, rejected, forgotten and abused like a pie dog. His school distanced him, the church mentally tortured him, society misused him, and a judge awarded him capital punishment to eliminate a hidden but lingering shame in his life. George Mooken and Parvathy stayed with their daughter in the USA, and Thoma Kunj forever missed their empathy and proximity. They might have abandoned their estate in Ayyankunnu or forgotten about Thoma Kunj forever, as he was sure if they had heard about him, they would have visited him at least once in gaol. But often, Thoma Kunj carried the images of Parvathy and George Mooken in his consciousness, and not knowing about them pained him. Thoma Kunj had never met people as unselfish as them, or he might have failed to understand them, as Parvathy and George Mooken remained a mystery in his heart.

Thoma Kunj learned there was nothing such as sincerity and commitment; people searched for their rewards, pleasures, and benefits. Humans were selfish. A greedy advocate impregnated Emily and awarded the death penalty to her son when he became a judge. The self-centred hostel warden protected a politician's son from infamy; she wanted to guard a young man's future, an MLA, MP, minister, governor, president, prime minister of the country or even a judge. Thoma Kunj was only a labourer, an unknown man who worked in a pigsty, someone who castrated pigs so that they would grow fast and earn more wealth for George Mooken.

Love was only a word without any meaning, its reverberations seemed endless, but in a sudden jerk, it disappeared like a magician's rope tricks. Humans loved to kill their love, hated it at a later stage, thought endlessly about eliminating it, and made complex plans to remove the love they once kept close to their hearts, and treasured hate for days, months, and years together. Love brought pain, agony, misery, disrepute, and conflicts as it possessed the person whom the person loved. In love, there was no freedom; possession was its ultimate sign. Akeem loved his concubines and paid a bag full of money to possess them, but he had no hesitation in beheading them when he hated them. Abraham wanted to sacrifice his only son Isaac to please his God, and God wanted to get the blood of humans once he created them with love. He threw those who refused to gratify him into eternal hell. Love was a myth, like a god.

Thoma Kunj was alone in this world, like the castrated Razak or a wounded baby bison. A predator could easily spot it and pounce upon it. He was unaccompanied, like a rejected calf, born to a single mother.

He castrated pigs; there was no one to protect the piglings from his knife, and he received a livelihood for gelding them. Akeem needed to spay Razak, as only a neutered Razak could be a waiter for his concubines. He induced Razak to be with him, and Razak had no other option; he was ignorant of Akeem and his Mashrabiya. Razak had no freedom; he was alone in Arabia, like a wounded baby camel amid the vast, endless wilderness. Razak had to lose his manhood to survive, and Akeem knew Razak's weak spot was his testes. God had superior testes to be a god, which he refused to give to humans; otherwise, humans would have castrated God. He enticed Akeem and millions of others worldwide with houris and wine, so they entered paradise to praise him.

The Merciful hated houris, so he created them without testicles. No one would have gone to paradise without houris, and there was no one to praise the Almighty. Without houris, there was no heaven.

On the remaining wall, Thoma Kunj painted the God of Abraham, Moses, Isaac, and Jacob, but he hated God. He reviled the God of Jesus, the God of the parish priest, who demanded a bribe to appoint Mama as a sweeper in a church-run school, where the government paid the salary. In his sermon on a Sunday, the vicar called Mama a "veshya", and Thoma Kunj loathed the God of the vicar, creating a vicar with testes. His abhorrence for God became infinite when the vicar refused to bury Mama in the church cemetery. George Mooken bribed the vicar, and he offered a bit of mire in the same cemetery where they had buried Papa.

In the paintings, God and the parish priest looked similar. Then Thoma Kunj painted Hell with Lucifer, and he looked like God; he was God.

The cell was a miniature hell, and the noose was at the entrance of hell.

The passage from the cell to the snare was narrow, with high walls on both sides. Many travelled through that, chained hands behind them. They were led to the gallows to fulfil a judge's wishes, as all decisions germinated as desires. Thoma Kunj had not yet travelled through that passage, and when he sauntered it, it would be his last journey. No one, not even a judge, could punish him after the executioner stiffened the noose with a knot over his gullet as he reached beyond all punishments. None could inflict any revenge or deterrence, and he would be a free man for the first time. Nobody was free in this world, as everyone carried the burden of existence. Thoma Kunj did not ask his mother to create him. After he was born, he knew he was made. Human freedom was a myth, a fable created by moralists, and they instilled that fairy tale in one and all with a false ego that boosted their desires and hallucinations. They applied it to others who were the underdogs, the oppressed, the subjugated and the powerless. The death penalty enhanced the self-image of a selected few, and they preached for hours about its paybacks so that they could increase their self-worth. Thoma Kunj did not try to lift his disposition as he knew who he was; he worked in a piggery, and all and sundry knew it. His mother was a sweeper, his father worked in the pigpen, and he followed his father's steps.

On the last wall, he painted pigs. They looked lovely with half-opened eyes that never looked at the sky, sun, moon, and stars. All were hidden, and the hogs could not see them; they did not exist for them. Something existed when someone knew it. The pigs had no god; all gods hated boars, and the pigs refused to accept a god. For them, God did not exist. Thoma Kunj drew his face among the pigs, and it looked like a hog, and he felt happy.

God created Adam in his image on the sixth day, and he felt happy. Thoma Kunj was the new Adam.

Thoma Kunj was happy to paint lovely piglets, their mothers and their fathers. They squealed and jumped up and down with joy because their mothers and fathers were delighted as they were free. In George Mooken's hog house, the shoats were castrated when they reached two to three weeks old, and every month there were about twenty piglets for castration. There were two boars for about forty sows and about four hundred piglets yearly. The pregnancy of a well-fed sow lasted three months and three days and produced eight to twelve piglets from each pregnancy.

A pig's life ended in a slaughterhouse, which was its final achievement or reward. But boars never committed a crime and obeyed their master as Razak obeyed Akeem, and the Egyptian doxy submitted to Akeem. Yet, Akeem beheaded her, and Padachon did not question him.

There was no abattoir in Thoma Kunj piggery on the wall, and the pigs celebrated their freedom. They did not sing and dance like the elites. They expressed joy in meeting others by touching each other with chubby faces and showering their affection. Appreciating the intimacy, an exclusive festivity, Thoma Kunj joined them and asked their forgiveness for castrating them. He knew he had done something terrible, unacceptable, the only crime he had committed. But the piglets were not revengeful; they did not award any deterrent punishment to him. He begged them not to leave him, and they celebrated his company with oinks.

The pigs snorted and walked around, touching Thoma Kunj as they were happy there was no guillotine to cut off their heads, and Thoma Kunj was thrilled as there were no gallows. There was no fear, no demeaning comments, and his pigs on the wall were excited, and for communication, they used body language and various grunts. There were soft and loud grunts; each had a different meaning as a sign of anticipation for food or pleasant company. A rough coughing noise showed the pig was annoyed or angry and shed tears with a murmur when a hog was sad or grieving.

When the piggery was started, George Mooken danced with the piglets, taking them on his shoulders, their legs protruding in front of his neck as he carried Parvathy. It was in August 1972, and it was raining heavily. He placed her around the back of his neck, walked from her coffee estate, and climbed the Western Ghats towards his village, about thirty kilometres. George Mooken was a bubbling young man active in ginger cultivation in Coorg; as its climate was better suited, the product far exceeded that of his village in Ayyankunnu. His parents migrated from Pala in 1947, and George was born in the same year. He had no siblings, and his parents died due to malaria when George was in the tenth grade.

Parvathy's father, Deva Moily, was against his daughter marrying a man from another state and a non-Coorgi, who belonged to a different religion and spoke an unlike language. He had plans for Parvathy to take over his flourishing coffee estate, which sold millions of rupees of coffee beans to international coffee companies every year. After the death of his son, Deva Moily was a depressed man and warned Parvathy he would shoot her if she dared cross the Lakshman Rekha, the bright-line rule. Like his father and grandfather, Deva Moily, a lieutenant colonel, was in the army under the British during the Second World War. He fought against the Japanese in Burma, lost his right leg, and spent six months in a military hospital in Calcutta before returning to Coorg and establishing his coffee estate. He had many guns, and hunting boars was his hobby.

Mooken hid in the coffee estate for four days, and on the last day, he jumped over the compound wall of the Moily mansion around three in the morning. As Parvathy had said, the outer gate guards were dozing; they were drugged. He walked through a long footpath within the garden and knew the guards who used to walk around the house, too, would be drugged. There was an outhouse whose door was not locked inside, and Mooken entered the structure without noise. Another corridor connected it with the main edifice.

The dogs were fast asleep, and so were Deva Moily and the servants.

George Mooken entered the mansion; Parvathy was waiting for him at the entrance of her bedroom. Her legs were chained, and she could walk only by taking short steps. Mooken lifted her and placed her around his neck like a large pigling. Parvathy had some food and water in her backpack.

Jumping over the compound wall was tough; it took more than half an hour to surmount. Then Mooken ambled through the coffee estate towards the forest. It was already four-thirty when they reached the rocks just below the hills, about three kilometres from Deva Moily's mansion. After resting behind the sarsens, Mooken took the chainsaw from his rucksack to cut the iron around Parvathy's ankle. But it was too hard to break.

Within ten minutes, they started climbing, Parvathy on his shoulders; there were steep hills with evergreen bushes, and a thick forest appeared after one hour. Mooken did not choose the beaten path of the hunters who hid here and there to gun down wild boars and bison. The climb was challenging, and Parvathy kept a profound silence. George Mooken did not stop and climb, holding spindly trees and hiding behind large ones. From the boulders, he had to climb around six kilometres and down for about eight to reach the Kerala border and, from there, about four kilometres to Attayoli and then four kilometres to his house in the village. He could feel the sun's first rays behind him within an hour, climbing one more hour. They rested between a rock and a massive tree while Parvathy opened her backpack.

They had Akki Otti, an unleavened flatbread of cooked rice with rice flour, crabs, tender bamboo shoots curry, baked monsoon mushrooms, and fried pork for breakfast. The water bottle in her bag quenched their thirst. By seven, they started again, Parvathy around George Mooken's back. They saw a lonely elephant near the bamboo growth about one hundred metres away from them by eight-thirty, and they hid behind a tree. After about half an hour, the elephant climbed towards a stream, and Mooken resumed his climb. Within an hour, they met a group of bison with calves crossing their path a little ahead of them. Once again, they stopped and leaned towards a tree. After a little while, they could hear some noise.

"There are hunters," Parvathy murmured in his ear.

"I can see them," George Mooken said.

They were chasing a pack of wild boars and shouting, four men and a woman, and all had guns.

"Hunting wild pig is common in Coorg; men and women go hunting. The whole night they are out in the bushes and within the forest," Parvathy said softly.

"Pork from wild boars is tasty," George said.

"I have some in the backpack," Parvathy whispered.

As the hunters were far, they started to climb. By the time they reached the peak, George was panting. It was eleven-twenty. They rested for a while and drank water. Parvathy had banana chips in her bag, and they munched on them for some time.

Climbing down was more arduous than climbing up, as George had to keep a steady balance. Sometimes, Parvathy on his shoulders was a blessing to maintain the equilibrium. There were more trees, bamboo growths and streams. More large animals roamed on the mountain's western slopes because of better rainfall and thick vegetation, and elephants in groups with young ones preferred such environments. A black bear appeared dangerously near them, and Mooken pulled out his revolver from his belt.

Around one in the afternoon, they rested within two massive rocks. Parvathy had several small packets within her backpack, steamed rice balls, wild boar pork called Pandi Curry, cooked thin rice strands known as

Noolputtu and chicken fry. After about twenty minutes, they resumed climbing down through the rain forest, and on the way, there were a large number of antelope called Nilgai and spotted deer known as Chital or Pulliman. Parvathy whispered they were in the northern periphery of the Nagarhole National Park, a tiger reserve.

The forest was alive with birds and animals, including grey langur, tiger, sloth bear, and elephant, and George Mooken sauntered carefully. Parvathy remained on his back, carefully maintaining her poise. Mooken started using a bamboo pole to climb down as it was dangerously steep for a long stretch. Around four in the evening, they reached the border of Kerala and at least one hour walk to Attayoli, the farmers' first settlements. The forest was so thick that it was impossible to see the sun, but George Mooken guessed it. Within half an hour, they reached the bushland with pythons, cobras, mongooses and peacocks; suddenly, they could see the sun precisely in front of them, a little above the western horizon.

Attayoli was marvellous. The church's steeples shone in the sun about three kilometres away, and the view was stupendous. There was greenery everywhere between houses, schools, hospitals, churches, temples, and mosques. About sixty-five kilometres away, the Arabian Sea appeared wrapped in blue mist.

The sun began to dip into the sea, and darkness permeated everywhere. George Mooken chose a narrow path to avoid farmers returning from the Angadikadavu bazaar.

"Paru, see, our house is about five hundred meters westwards of the church," Mooken said while walking steadily.

"I can see the church," said Parvathy. "How long will it take from here?"

"We shall be home within forty minutes," replied Mooken.

They rested in a vast cashew plantation for a while, and then Mooken walked briskly. He was anxious to reach home without exposing them to the public. They entered a rubber estate without any undergrowth, and the walking turned easy. The coconut plantation by the side of the church was slightly marshy. Darkness spread everywhere, like the monsoon clouds within the coffee estate. Parvathy lit her torch, and Mooken could see where to place his next step. When they reached home, it was about eight-fifteen.

"Paru, we are home," George said with excitement. His deep palpitation was visible.

"George," Parvathy called and hugged him.

"Thank you, dear, for coming with me. We have already started our life together. Love you for your trust," said Mooken kissing her cheeks.

"Let me thank you for your love; you walked about thirty kilometres climbing on the Western Ghats, passing through challenging terrain amid dangerous wild animals. We will remember this day till our deaths and tell our children to celebrate the day in remembrance of our love," Parvathi said.

"Yes, my Paru. Together we conquered it; coolly, we will go forward," Mooken replied.

He led Parvathy inside, and with an electric saw, he cut the chain from both ankles.

"Let us keep it as a memory of the bondage we confronted, the struggle we endured, the determination we expressed to break it, our trust in each other, and our eternal love," said Parvathy, taking the broken pieces of the iron.

It was a small house with two bedrooms, a large sitting room, and a kitchen with an attached dining hall. They cooked dinner together.

Paru and George discussed their marriage the next day, and Mooken said he preferred a Hindu wedding.

"George, I desire to have a wedding in the church; let us converse with the parish priest and fix a date," Parvathy expressed her desire.

"Paru, your happiness is mine too," said Mooken, hugging Parvathy.

They went to the church in the evening, discussed with the parish priest, and fixed the marriage for the following day. Mooken invited ten of his immediate neighbours for the ceremony and the party.

Parvathy wore a Mysore silk saree, and George, his grey suit with a red tie. The ceremony was simple, and the party was in their house.

In the evening, around four, abruptly, there was a roaring sound in the courtyard of their house. About ten jeeps and about seventy-five men jumped out of them and circled the house like a pack of mountain wolves surrounding a bison. All of them had guns in their hands.

Then Deva Moily entered the sitting room with a revolver. "Parvathy!" he thundered. It was like the roaring of a wounded tiger in the Mysore Zoo.

"Kill me instead of my Parvathy," George pleaded, prostrating before Moily.

Moily kicked his face with his boots.

"You rascal, how dare you steal my daughter from me," Moily bellowed, aiming his gun toward Mooken.

"Papa, please forgive me!" It was Parvathy, kneeling before her father. She put her hands around his legs and moaned.

Moily stood still. Parvathy was in her Mysore silk saree, and Moily remembered Sobhana, his wife, who always wore a silk saree and died after a bear attack five years ago.

"Sobhana," Moily cried, throwing his revolver. He lifted his daughter by her shoulders and hugged her. "Parvathy, I could never do this," said Moily and wept like a child.

"Send all your children to Coorg as soon as they reach two years. They will grow under my care; I will educate them in the best schools and colleges in Mysore and Bangalore. They don't belong to you, but me alone. They will inherit my wealth. Under these conditions, I spare this man's life," Moily roared, pointing the gun towards Mooken.

"Yes, Papa, I agree," Parvathy said.

"You are welcome to the estate, but this man should never set foot over there. This is an order," Moily said before marching forward.

"In that case, I will never go there," Parvathy replied.

Parvathy and George Mooken celebrated their freedom in the quietness of their house. She was meticulous in her planning and had lengthy discussions with her husband.

They planted better-yielding varieties of rubber saplings on ten acres, cashew on the hillslopes for fifteen acres, and coconut trees for five acres. There was a variety of mango, jackfruit and other fruit trees. The cattle shed they developed on the riverside was the most modern, with five Jersey cows from Munnar, three Brown Sahiwal cows from South Canara, and two Haryanvi buffalos. The goats from Kutch, Rajasthan and UP multiplied every six months, and the poultry farm was thriving. Land measuring three acres was earmarked for a piggery next to the barn.

Every year for one month, George Mooken and Parvathi spent their holidays abroad, and within fifteen years, they had visited all countries in Europe and the Americas. Mooken's interest was animal husbandry and agriculture during his visits. Parvathy collected seeds of trees from Scandinavia, Eastern and Western Europe, Canada, the USA, and Latin American countries to plant on their farm in Ayyankunnu.

A child was born within one year of marriage, and Parvathy and George called her Anupriya. On her third birthday, Deva Moily sent two nurses and two security guards to Ayyankunnu to get the child. The parents cried bitterly but had to send the baby to her grandfather. Anupriya grew up in Coorg and played in the courtyard of Deva Moily. She completely forgot about her parents and learned the local Kodagu, Kannada and English fluently without knowing a single word in Malayalam. Anupriya studied in the best schools in Mysore, where the classes were in Kannada and English. Parvathy and George Mooken never got an opportunity to talk to their daughter. They regularly went to Mysore and stood outside the gate of Anupriya's school to glance at their daughter. But for Anupriya, her parents were strangers.

Within ten years of their marriage, Parvathy and George constructed a new house, a mansion.

After fifteen years of the birth of Anupriya, Parvathy and George Mooken had another child named Anupama. On the third birthday of Anupama, a jeep came from Coorg with two nurses and two security guards. Parvathy and George Mooken cried loudly and ran after the jeep for a couple of kilometres. Anupama started crying for days in her grandfather's manor and refused to eat.

Anupama was sent back to Ayyankunnu to be with her parents within a week. The nurses and guards landed again on the eight-day and took Anupama to her grandfather. Even though Anupama stopped crying, she suffered from a fever and cough for two weeks. Once again, she was sent back to Parvathy, and after fifteen days, the nurses and guards arrived to pick her up.

On the third time, Anupama stayed with her grandfather for three months, but she was moody, lonely and sad. She refused to be a part of the Moily family. Anupama was sent back to Ayyankunnu and stayed with her parents until her next birthday. On her fourth birthday, once again, the nurses and guards appeared. Even though she was reluctant, Anupama had to go with the retinue. Soon, she was admitted to a kindergarten near the estate, and every day, Deva Moily accompanied her and remained with her till the classes were over.

Meanwhile, after completing her MBA in coffee plantation management, Anupriya joined her grandfather's coffee estate as the CEO. She extended the coffee plantation for another three hundred acres within five years. She acquired shares of coffee estates in different parts of Coorg, formed a consortium with like-minded coffee estate owners and signed an agreement with a Swiss company to supply sufficient coffee seeds for their coffee bean-crushing plant in Coorg. Her grandfather was proud of Anupriya and often told her she was as beautiful and intelligent as her grandmother.

During her school days, Anupama visited her parents once a month, and besides Kodagu, Kannada, and English, she learned to read and write in Malayalam. She went to the church with them, joined the choir, and visited many families with carol singers during Christmas. Anupama attended school in Mysore and stayed with her parents on weekends after driving up to Ayyankunnu. She adored her parents and loved to be with them always.

One evening, Anupriya suddenly appeared in Ayyankunnu. She was there for the first time, and Parvathy and George Mooken found it hard to recognise her as they had never had an opportunity to talk to her before. Anupriya told Parvathy that her grandfather had arranged her marriage, and the groom was an officer in the army. Her grandfather told her for the first time that her mother stayed with her husband in a remote corner of Malabar. And Anupriya was there to invite her mother to attend the wedding.

"Your father is also here; I am not alone," said Parvathy to Anupriya.

"How could you run away with such a bugger?" shouted Anupriya.

"How dare you abuse your father, bloody bitch!" Parvathy shouted, slapping Anupriya in the face.

Blood oozed from her mouth.

"He is your father. Without him, you would not have been born; get out of my house, never come back," Parvathy roared and shooed off Anupriya.

After completing her senior secondary school, Anupama joined IIT Madras and, with her parents, visited many countries and famous universities during her vacations.

Anupama and Anupriya were strangers and never cared to talk to each other, even though their grandfather tried his best to make them friends.

After graduating, Anupama went to the USA and joined an Ivy League university for her postgraduation in Artificial Intelligence. Within two years, she registered for a doctorate in microsystems engineering at a university in California. Parvathy and George Mooken visited their daughter every six months, and Anupama cherished their company. When she got a job in a well-known company, Anupama invited her parents to migrate to the USA and stay with her, and for Parvathy and George Mooken, the invite was enticing. Soon Anupama started her start-up, which grew into a highly successful venture with branches in many countries. Parvathy and George Mooken decided to go to the US to spend their old age with their daughter. They asked Thoma Kunj to look after their estate as his own in their absence or till they returned and informed all workers of their decision.

Thoma Kunj looked at the picture of Parvathy on his wall in astonishment. She was courageous and deeply in love with her husband for all the moments of her life. George Mooken was a lucky man; he went through hell and carried her on his shoulders to his home like a precious stone. He did not allow her to gait and never looked back. But Orpheus was not that lucky; he went to the Netherworld to bring back his beloved wife, Eurydice, to the world of the living. Hades agreed under the condition that Eurydice had to follow behind him while walking out from the Underworld, and Orpheus could not turn to look back at her till they crossed the final gate. Just Orpheus walked out of the outer gate; he turned around and gazed at the face of Eurydice. But alas, she had not yet crossed the boundary of the land of the dead; she disappeared into eternal death.

George Mooken was wise, carried his beloved, and did not need to look back. Parvathy was always with him as one body and one spirit.

But Thoma Kunj was not wise because he chose silence and refused to defend himself. He carried others' crimes on his shoulders. The noose waited for him at the end of the chasm.

The Superintendent had already stepped outside the cell. Thoma Kunj followed him with the jailors on both sides, the guard behind him; the parade started.

Chapter Three

THE PARADE

The parade entered a long corridor, which extended to the gallows. There were two such access strips, one for the convict to be hanged and the other for dignitaries, the district magistrate or a bureaucrat appointed by the government, who witnessed the hanging to verify and report to the government that the correct prisoner received the death penalty. The path looked similar, but the purpose was different but not obscure. The notables came from different backgrounds and imposed laws that protected them by eliminating perceived threats. They were the progenies of Hammurabi and Bentham.

Those who made the law escaped from its murkier galleries. The law treated the voiceless, powerless, oppressed, subjugated, and dark-skinned harshly, with revenge and retribution. Those in power silenced others. Thoma Kunj was silent, with no parent, relatives, friends or God. He was a rejected man, lonely but straightforward.

As the President of India in the Republic Day parade, Thoma Kunj was at the centre of the procession.

It was a silent cavalcade, except for the heavy footsteps of the prison personnel.

Thoma Kunj was barefooted, having lost his freedom to wear footwear. He walked without any support from the guards, as he had no fear, hope, or hatred. On several other occasions, the guards had to carry the condemned as many fell unconscious; some refused to walk as if the noose could be prevented by declining to tread. Many might cry loudly, howl, or lament; some could not accept fate, shout in an incoherent language like a Pentecostal preacher, and plead for God's mercy and intervention. A few urinated with fear.

The final struggle was to save one's breath by avoiding the noose, but the scaffolds were an inevitable truth; there was no exit from it.

Accepting the facts of life as they were, Thoma Kunj overcame sorrows and pains.

It wasn't very sensible to convince the judge, as he had already decided the case. The trial was a sham, and he realised that the witnesses had a prepared text to narrate. Thoma Kunj had only ever seen three witnesses out of the six before.

Thoma Kunj was confident he would be acquitted as he had done no wrong, and the judge would realise his inculpability, even before the trial. The incidents were so simple and forthright. Thoma Kunj went to the hostel around three in the afternoon; it was his first visit. After parking his bike in the parking bay, he walked up to the main entrance and pressed the calling bell. An attendant appeared; she might have been fifty to fifty-five years old; Thoma Kunj told her that the hostel warden had called him to repair the leaking pipe. He explained to her he was from George Mooken's pig farm, and Mooken had asked him if he had to go to the hostel to do urgent plumbing work. The attendant took him to the hostel warden, whose office was next to the entrance. He stood at the room entrance, and the attendant knocked on the door; after some time, the warden opened her door and came out. Thoma Kunj repeated his story to the warden, who looked serious. She was a tall, lean woman with a pair of spectacles; her grey hair was prominent. The warden explained the nature of work on the terrace of their three-storied hostel building. The leakage was from the pipe which connected to the water tank.

The hostel warden directed the attendant to take Thoma Kunj to the terrace of the building. They climbed the stairs; the building was at least thirty years old and kept somewhat shabby and dirty. Thoma Kunj followed the attendant. There was a door at the end of the stairs; the attendant opened it, and Thoma Kunj and the attendant entered a frowzy and untidy terrace and in one of its corners was the water tank.

The water tank was made of laterite brownstone blocks and cement; the plaster had peeled off from many places, exposing the stones. But the leakage was not severe, and no urgent mending was required; only a few drops of water were visible from the pipeline joints. He was sure the plumber of the hostel would have seen it.

Thoma Kunj finished the work within half an hour, and the leakage stopped entirely. As soon as he had joined the piggery at the age of fourteen, mainly to castrate piglings, he started doing the plumbing and electrical work in many of the buildings of George Mooken for an additional income. But he had never gone to any other place to do plumbing or electrical work, and it was the first time he went out to do plumbing. He went to the hostel only because of the instruction of George Mooken that he could not reject. Thoma Kunj was aware that Parvathy and George Mooken were going to America on the same afternoon to be with their daughter for an indefinite period. On the previous day, they had called Thoma Kunj to their home, and during dinner, they asked him to look after their estate till they returned. It meant they would be with their daughter Anupama, and there was little possibility of returning to Ayyankunnu in their old age. Parvathy and George Mooken gave a sealed envelope to Thoma Kunj, saying it contained a will, a registered legal document that the estate would belong to Thoma Kunj after their death. Reaching home, Thoma Kunj kept it in his steel cupboard.

After completing the work, he looked down from the terrace. The hostel had a vast compound, at least four acres of land, filled with scrubs and creepers. The garden in front of the hostel was equally scruffy. There were a few old or dead coconut trees without leaves, here and there like discarded smokestacks that he had seen in a cashew nut factory near Thalassery. The whole compound looked fiendish, and Thoma Kunj wondered how women could stay there comfortably and peacefully.

About twenty metres from the main building, a well was overshadowed by bushes and covered with creepers. Thoma Kunj noticed an iron staircase from the terrace to the ground outside the hostel building.

The attendant did not wait for Thoma Kunj; she had already gone without telling him. He opened the door from the promenade and climbed down the stairs alone. The hostel was almost empty, and there was silence everywhere, like in a cemetery. The hostellers must have gone for a short vacation. He felt awful about the physical condition of the building as the plastering had peeled off in numerous places, and water diffusion during the monsoon was visible on the walls with large diabolic images.

When Thoma Kunj returned to the office of the hostel warden, she asked him to examine the water level and the position of immersed water pump within the well. She could have verified it by looking at the well, and her request did not serve any purpose for Thoma Kunj or the hostel, as she told him he could go back after inspecting the well. He wondered why she did not want to get a report from him about the water quantity and the pump's location. Besides, she did not pay him for his work, which he found atypical. It might have been because she contacted George Mooken directly and made the payment. But Parvathy and Mooken had already left for Calicut airport to take a flight to Doha and Washington Dulles International Airport in the afternoon. They would be staying with Anupama for an extended period.

As on the previous day, Mooken had called Thoma Kunj a week ago and requested him to look after his property during his absence, maintain the accounts, pay the labourers, and supervise the farm's work, including the cowsheds and pigsty. Whenever they went out, Thoma Kunj managed all their work. It was a big responsibility, and Thoma Kunj was honest about his work with George Mooken and Parvathy. They trusted him, and they had some plans for him.

As he had seen the well from the terrace of the building, he went alone to find out the water level and to trace the position of the submerged water pump that impelled drinking water to the overhead tank. He went through an internal corridor and a door by the side of the kitchen leading towards the courtyard. A pump house was there by the side of the well, which was dilapidated.

Thoma Kunj leaned against the rounded wall of the well. The laterite stone blocks were dangerously wobbly; many stones had already fallen in the well, and some were on the ground. As it was the peak of the monsoon, there was plenty of water in the well, and he thought he could touch it; he extended his right hand inside the well. But the water was further below. As he leaned, a couple of stones fell into the water, making a splash so loud that the dog in the kennel started barking loudly. The cook from the kitchen ran out, and her face showed she was visibly upset with the noise.

"What happened? Has something fallen in the well?" She asked.

"A few stones have fallen," said Thoma Kunj.

"Then why are you leaning towards the well?" she questioned again.

"Just looking at the well to find out the depth of water and the location of the immersed pump," Thoma Kunj answered with slight embarrassment.

"No, I cannot believe you," saying she came near Thoma Kunj and looked inside the well.

"I told you the truth," said Thoma Kunj. He knew that the explanation given to her was rather foolish.

"It was something weighty; the water is still buoyant," she said.

"Why don't you believe me?" Thoma Kunj questioned.

She looked at Thoma Kunj for a few minutes and went back.

There was undergrowth and creepers within the inner wall of the well. It was impossible to see the immersed pump's position as it was deep, having at least twenty feet of water. Thoma Kunj spent two minutes there and then walked to the parking bay. He could see a face watching him from the window of the hostel entrance but could not recognise the person. Thoma Kunj started his bike and went out.

But Thoma Kunj felt terrible as the woman doubted him. She might have thought he was lying as something else fell in the water.

On the first day of the trial, the judge asked whether Thoma Kunj had a lawyer to defend him. He replied he could not afford a lawyer. After a pause, he said the case was so simple that he could explain it and did not need a lawyer. Besides, he was not interested in defending. The judge told him the court could appoint a lawyer free of cost to protect him. Once again, Thoma Kunj informed the judge he could explain the truth as he did not believe in defending himself. In this world, everyone should defend everyone else.

Thoma Kunj did not give any importance to the meaning of the word defending in a trial court, as he thought he could explain what exactly happened to the judge. He did not care that the prosecutor would ask various questions based on the incident following the Indian Penal Code, Criminal Procedure Code, and the Evidence Act. Thoma Kunj was ignorant that it was an evidence-based trial, not a truth-based one. The public prosecutor could establish rape and murder charges against him based on evidence given by the witnesses and not on the truth or what exactly had happened.

Thoma Kunj thought about Appu, the physical torture Thoma Kunj suffered in the headmaster's cabin, and the oath he took in Emily's name that he would never defend himself in any situation. He did not care that questioning in the headmaster's cabin and the evidence-based trial in a criminal court were two separate realities. In a court, some incidents lacked evidence, even though they were true, and no one could deny it but fail as evidence. So, the truth could be dismissed during a trial in a trial court. Incidents were either true or false, and there was no debate. There were only actual incidents in Thoma

Kunj's world, and there could not be any false events, as falsity could not exist. For him, what occurred was the reality, and its veracity was beyond all trials.

After many days of trial, when the judge pronounced the verdict, Thoma Kunj realised it was an unfair trial, and the judgment was bogus. According to the court, evidence could not exist outside the realm of facts unearthed; it must be seen, heard, touched, tasted or smelt. Suppose a person did not know a flower in the forest that did not exist. Thoma Kunj was surprised to learn the new definition of actuality, post-truth. He was under the impression that something existed without knowledge or evidence. But for the trial court, the fact was an experienced reality.

So, it happened as evidenced when the public prosecutor and the witnesses said that Thoma Kunj raped the minor, strangulated her and dumped her body in the well. Many asserted that it happened and became a truth by changing its definition. But Thoma Kunj could not accept it, as the incidents cited with evidence did not occur.

In the trial, the judge explained the ground rules to be followed in court. Suddenly, Thoma Kunj became the defendant. The public prosecutor gave an opening statement containing the case's core: Thoma Kunj went to the women's hostel, raped a minor girl in one of the rooms, strangulated her and finally dumped her body in the well.

Thoma Kunj had no lengthy statement to make. He told the court he went to the hostel directed by George

Mooken, met with the warden, and repaired the leaking pipeline as requested. Once again, he went to the warden to report that he had completed the work. Then he walked up to the well to see the water level as the warden asked him to do and the location of the immersed pump. Finally, he returned home.

Thoma Kunj did not take the trial seriously as he never thought it would affect his life; he could be punished for a crime he did not commit. He could not imagine being awarded the death penalty and going for appeal again. And when the final appeal was rejected, he would be taken to the gallows. The trial was like a one-act play; he thought he played in the school where he was a character. After the one-act play, he wore his school uniform and returned home in the evening. He believed he would return home, engage in his everyday work on the pig farm, and look after the estate in the absence of Parvathy and George Mooken as they had gone to the US.

There were no witnesses from the side of Thoma Kunj, as he was under the impression that he alone was sufficient as he refused to defend the case. It was unnecessary to have a witness, as no one knew about his going to the women's hostel except Parvathy and George Mooken, who went to their daughter in the United States. Thoma Kunj trusted the truth of what exactly happened in the working women's hostel on that Sunday. He thought the judge would believe him when he explained the simple facts. The truth was simple, it was clear like the sunlight, and there was no doubt about it. It was what happened; it was not that did not occur, and there was no dispute about it, as what did not happen did not exist. It was like everyone saying that the sun was the sun and the moon was the moon, as the sun could not be the moon, and the moon could not be the sun.

A trial in a criminal case was meaningless as there was nothing to argue or verify, and Thoma Kunj questioned the purpose of a trial in his mind. Evidence could create falsehood, and the truth would be buried somewhere during the trial or at its end. Evidence was the deciding factor, and the public prosecutor could make it, and a naive judge could believe it, or he could become a party to weave tales.

The judge was the deciding factor in a criminal trial. He could be with the truth or against it. He could float on the waves created by the public prosecutor and suppress the facts based on false evidence or stand with the truth rejecting false evidence.

The truth represented reality, which was the opposite of a lie, and untruth could not exist because it lacked self-vibration and inner potentiality. The truth was related to experience, but it was nothing but fact; a witness could not change it. As falsehood could not change the truth, truth always supported another truth and understood the next one. The truth was categorical, and when it was spoken, it asserted specific facts, beliefs, and statements that supported each other, and there was no contradiction. Emily, his mother, was the truth, and so was his father, Kurien, who loved him. That he burned all pictures of the Sacred Heart of Jesus, the Virgin Mary, and all saints was a truth. The nonexistence of God was the truth. All people had specific knowledge and beliefs that their world was the truth.

Thoma Kunj could not think of an untruth as he always spoke the truth. His mother and father taught him to tell the truth. And when he told the court he did not see the girl, did not rape her, did not strangulate her, and did not dump her body in a well, what he spoke was the truth. And he did not know why he should ask a lawyer to defend him in a trial. Thoma Kunj was his lawyer, as he could tell the truth. But he failed to understand why he should convince a judge what he said was authentic. It was the duty of the police to find out who the rapist was, who had murdered the minor girl, strangulated her and dumped her in a well. An innocent person had no role in it, and Thoma Kunj refused to appoint a lawyer and did not accept a court-appointed lawyer to defend him. He didn't need to protect himself because convincing someone about his innocence harmed another person, as everyone was responsible for everyone.

The public prosecutor was weaving a false story, and Thoma Kunj assumed the judge would reject it as his job was searching for the truth. The public prosecutor was clear and consistent in his presentation of events. He was logical and produced evidence after evidence based on a solid foundation that challenged the guiltlessness of Thoma Kunj. But what the public prosecutor spoke was untruth even though supported by evidence. The evidence became the antithesis of fact, leading Thoma Kunj to the scaffolds.

The witnesses were the hostel warden, the attendant, the cook, and three unknown persons. Their story was built on a solid logical foundation created by interlocked tiles of the Indian Penal Code and the Evidence Act woven and pronounced by the public prosecutor. They looked like the actual truth, but the witnesses were verisimilitude robots.

The first witness was the attendant. She looked different in a saree, but Thoma Kunj recognised her. She said in court that she opened the door after the defendant rang the bell and led the accused to the hostel warden. After getting orders from the warden, she took the defendant to the terrace through the internal staircase. She noticed the defendant was curious and carefully observed the walls and ground. Reaching just below the terrace, she opened the door from the inside, which was always kept locked. On the terrace, she showed the defendant the work, and he immediately started the job, but he never talked to her. After two minutes, she left him and went down without locking the door from the inside, as the defendant would be coming down to meet with the warden to inform her about the work. The defendant returned within thirty minutes, and she saw the defendant entering the hostel warden's room. She did not remain with the hostel warden and the defendant because she had other work and was unaware of what happened afterwards.

The judge told the defendant as he had no lawyer to represent him, he could question the witness. Thoma Kunj did not ask anything of the witness as what the witness had said in the court was true for the witness, and he did not want to examine the witness.

"Why are you silent?" asked the judge.

"It is my right to be silent?" replied Thoma Kunj.

"You are the accused," said the judge.

"For them, I am the accused, but for me, I am innocent," said Thoma Kunj.

"You need to protect yourself," said the judge.

"They must protect me by not falsely accusing me, as I don't accuse anyone. It is impossible to reply to all accusations, and I don't react to any of them," replied Thoma Kunj.

The judge laughed.

The next witness was a young man who had problems walking as if he had suffered from polio. He told the court he had been the sweeper in the hostel for the past ten years. As a teenager, he went there and worked, helped the cook, and ran errands for the hostel warden. He usually started the pump every morning at five and evening at six. In a small room under the staircase on the hostel's ground floor, he stayed and was a bachelor. As an orphan, he had nowhere to go during the holidays.

It was around four-forty-five afternoon on a Sunday. He was taking a rest in his room, listening to film songs. Suddenly he heard someone crying. It was the voice of a young girl; as he had been in the women's hostel for more than ten years, he could recognise women's voices. But it was a girl's cry, and he opened the door and entered the corridor. Once again, there was a faint cry. It was from a room on the ground floor, he was sure. He frantically searched for the room and found a room locked from the inside. He knew a girl was staying in her sister's room. She came to the hostel in the morning, not knowing her sister had gone home the previous day. The girl waited in her room as the evening bus to her town was around five.

He knocked at the door, and no one opened it. But he was sure the girl was there in the room. He ran towards the hostel warden's office, but she was not there and searched for her and found her in the garden after about twenty minutes. Informing her about the incident, he ran towards the girl's room. The hostel warden ran ahead of him. When they entered the corridor, it was about five in the evening, and he saw the defendant carrying the girl in his arms and running through the corridor. The defendant opened the door by the side of the kitchen but could not see the warden following him. When the witness reached the doorstep, he saw the defendant leaning towards the well.

"I did not see his face, but I had his side view. I am sure the defendant was the person who was running with the body of the girl," said the witness. The prosecutor requested the judge to note the event in their sequence, and the typist typed every word of the witness.

Thoma Kunj had a surprised look listening to what the sweeper was saying. It was an untruth.

The judge asked the defendant whether he wanted to question the witness. Thoma Kunj said what the witness said about him, and the narrated events were false. He did not enter the girl's room and never knew the girl the witness was talking about. Thoma Kunj had never seen the girl, and there was no question of raping, strangulating, running with her body through the corridor and dumping it in the well.

Thoma Kunj refused to question the witness as he believed by examining the witness, he could not change the untruth uttered by the witness.

How will you prove that you are innocent?" asked the judge.

"Why should I prove I am innocent? I am innocent, and it is a fact. But I don't want to prove to everyone who makes false accusations about me. It is humanly impossible for me to stop people from saying falsehoods. It is my right not to react to falsehood," said Thoma Kunj.

"It is you who are the accused. Only disproving what the witness told you could prove you are guiltless," The judge said.

"I am. Why do I need external proof affirming my inculpability?" Replied Thoma Kunj.

"I need evidence; I am not searching for truth. Evidence can refute an untruth. Your silence, self-righteousness, and simplicity will be insufficient in a trial court. You must protect yourself from dangers to your life," explained the judge.

"I don't believe in a trial which is not based on categorical truth," replied Thoma Kunj.

The judge laughed.

The next witness was the gardener of the hostel. He said he had stayed in an old two-room shack on the hostel premises with his wife and two children for six years. On Sundays, he had no work, but he often walked around the hostel garden. Around five-twenty, he heard a commotion near the well, ran towards it and saw the defendant tossing a girl's body in the well. The hostel warden was just outside the door, next to the kitchen, and the sweeper was behind her. There was a splashing sound from the well. The cook came out running, and she shouted at the defendant, asking what he was doing. The defendant did not utter a word; he was silent. The gardener said he was frightened to see the face of the defendant. Soon he started his bike and went out as if nothing had happened.

Thoma Kunj looked at the gardener in surprise. He was confident in his narration as if it had happened. But the gardener was dishonest; there was nothing which he said was true.

Once again, the judge repeated whether the defendant was interested in questioning the witness. Thoma Kunj told the judge what the witness said was pure imagination. Even though the witness uttered a lie, Thoma Kunj was not interested in questioning the witness, as a lie cannot be converted into a truth.

The gatekeeper of the hostel was the next witness, a hefty man, about six feet tall, around forty years old.

He had been with the women's hostel for the previous twelve years. There were two more gatekeepers, each working for eight hours every day. Whenever a person took leave, others worked for twelve hours. On Sunday, he started his work at six in the morning. The defendant reached the hostel around three in the afternoon, and the gatekeeper asked him to park his bike in the parking bay for two-wheelers. He asked the defendant why he was there, and the defendant told him he was there to meet the warden to do some repair work. Then the defendant went inside. Around five-twenty, there was a loud noise from the well, and he could hear some people shouting and crying. He ran towards the well, and the defendant was standing near the well. The hostel warden was outside the kitchen door, and the sweeper was behind her. The gardener was standing looking inside the well. The cook came running and asked the defendant what he was doing, why there was a noise and a few more questions. The gatekeeper could recognise the defendant's face as he had asked him to park his bike in the parking bay for two-wheelers.

Then the public prosecutor asked whether he could identify the defendant. The gatekeeper said loudly, "yes," and turned towards Thoma Kunj and told the court that he was the person he was talking about and he was the person who was standing near the well.

Thoma Kunj felt like laughing as he knew the gatekeeper was lying. But he thought he was not serious; the whole court drama was a one-act play, and he would go home after the play. Thoma Kunj could not realise the seriousness of the trial, which he thought a child's play.

The judge gave another chance to Thoma Kunj to question the witness, and Thoma Kunj told the judge what the witness said in court was an untruth that had never happened. Besides, he had never seen the witness before and did not want to question someone who told lies in court.

The following witness was the cook. She told the court that there was a big commotion outside the kitchen near the well, so she ran outside to see what was happening. The hostel warden and the sweeper were already there. The gardener was looking into the well.

The witness asked the defendant what had happened and whether something had fallen in the well. The defendant replied some stones had fallen in the well. Then the witness asked why the defendant was leaning towards the well, and he replied he was looking into the well to find out the water lever and the location of the immersed pump. The witness said she could not believe the defendant, as something hefty had fallen in the well, and the water had risen. The witness told the court the defendant looked like he was hiding something. A couple of stones falling would not have made such noise. The noise was because the defendant had thrown a heavy object into the well.

The judge asked whether the defendant wanted to question the witness. Thoma Kunj replied to the judge he declined to question the witness, but he wished to comment on what the witness had said. The judge allowed him to make the comments. The defendant said what the witness said about him was true, but what the witness said about other witnesses was untrue.

The public prosecutor said the defendant accepted the witness's statement by refusing to question the witness.

The last witness was the hostel warden. She wore a white cotton saree and a full-sleeved blouse. Around fifty-five years old, she looked impressive, with her grey hair neatly combed and tied behind her head. The spectacles' frame was silver, and her voice was slow but loud and clear as if she was speaking from an earthen jar, albeit her face was expressionless; there were no emotional variations in her sound. In the beginning, she narrated the incidents in the third person.

The defendant came to the hostel around three-twenty in the afternoon. The warden explained the nature of the work Thoma Kunj had to complete. Along with the hostel attendant, he went up to the terrace to fix the leakage in the pipeline on the overhead tank. The attendant returned immediately, and the defendant completed the work within half an hour. The defendant was paid for his work, and the warden asked him to leave. Then the warden started talking about the victim.

She was a fifteen-year-old schoolgirl who reached the hostel around eight-thirty in the morning to meet her sister, a hosteller. The girl was a boarder in a school about two kilometres from the working women's hostel.

On some occasions, with the permission of her school headmistress, she visited her sister to spend Sundays with her and returned to her school the next day early in the morning. That day, she went to the hostel to travel with her sister to their home for a seven-day holiday, not knowing her sister had already gone. There was a direct bus to her hometown around five in the evening, which reached her hometown within two hours, so the girl waited in her sister's room alone. While walking through the hostel's corridor, the defendant saw the girl; he entered her room, raped her, and strangulated her.

Hearing the noise within the room, the sweeper of the hostel rushed to the room. It was locked from the inside. He could listen to feeble cries from the room. Then he ran up to the warden's room to inform her.

Suddenly the warden changed the narration to the first person.

"The sweeper met me in the garden and told me about the noise in the girl's room. Along with him, I hurried inside the hostel building. I saw the defendant running through the corridor carrying the girl's body. His face was visible. He was the defendant. It was around five-fifteen, and the defendant was in the girl's room for about half an hour. I ran after him shouting, but he opened the door and went out and flung the body of the girl into the well. The gardener was already there, and the gatekeeper came running, then the cook."

The defendant raped the girl, strangulated her, carried her body in his hand, went to the well, and hurled it in.

Thoma Kunj looked at the warden in disbelief. What she said was an untruth. The hostel warden knew she was lying, but she projected what she said was true.

The judge asked Thoma Kunj whether he wanted to examine the witness. Thoma Kunj told the judge that almost everything the witness had said was false. He did not want to question her, as falsehood could never become true. She had a right to say what she wanted, but at the same time, she had a duty to tell the truth. But she failed miserably as her evidence was not factual.

The truth was sincere, genuine and honest, and it did not need a test or evidence to be the truth. Only those who were afraid of others defended themselves. The one who trusted in oneself stood alone, and Thoma Kunj stood alone. Fearless, he accepted anything that happened. But he challenged everything that contradicted the actual, even though he failed to convince the judge, who was already convinced by his history. He wanted to erase that history forever, and the trial was a chimaera for others. When the baby was growing in the womb, he pleaded with the mother to abort it, as its birth would affect his law practice and his future. But the woman refused to oblige.

It was sheer coincidence Thoma Kunj's case was tried in his court. He knew the innocence of Thoma Kunj, but he did not want to carry the burden of his infatuation with a young woman.

Kurien never asked about the woman's antecedents he met in the Jubilee Park at Kottayam. Her baby was born in his aunt's place. He married her, went with her to a distant land, and worked in a piggery. Kurien loved Thoma Kunj like his own son.

Thoma Kunj did not commit homicide, as he did not rape and asphyxiate the girl. The judge did not accept what Thoma Kunj said as he believed in what the public prosecutor said. The public prosecutor wanted to win his case as the MLA was his friend; besides, the judge wanted to erase his past. They both had different objectives to achieve, not knowing each other's motives.

It was not Thoma Kunj's responsibility to counter all arguments, exposing the falsehood of others. He had the right to keep silent, not defend, and he did not believe in defending himself. He did not see the minor girl, and it was a fact. If the judge refused to accept the point, it was not Thoma Kunj's fault, as the judge failed to know the truth and messed up in finding out the actual rapist. It was not Thoma Kunj's duty to search and find the rapist, as it was the duty of the police.

Thoma Kunj imagined the judge could read his inculpability easily as he searched for facts and indications. The judge's duty was to pronounce a verdict based on facts, and Thoma Kunj had no obligation to enlighten the judge. If the judge delivered a wrong judgment, it would show his incapability to provide justice. Selfish people defended themselves, and unwise judges gave an incorrect verdict. Thoma Kunj did not have a selfish motive to live. His effort was to lead a sincere life without hurting others. As he was not the reason for his life, he had no reason to defend his life, even though everyone's life was precious to one and all.

The public prosecutor told the court that all the witnesses had seen the defendant, and two of them had seen him carrying the minor girl's body and throwing it in the well. Two of them had seen him leaning towards the well; all six had heard a loud noise from the well when the minor girl's body fell into the water. All six witnesses were sure the defendant had committed the crimes. The defendant raped, strangulated, and killed the minor girl. Then he tossed her body into the well. He was afraid to question witnesses as he was scared to face the evidence, and he could not prove anything false in the arguments of the witnesses.

With its various sections and intricacies of the criminal laws and the complexities of the evidence act, the public prosecutor created a world where he bestowed Thoma Kunj the title of a rapist and murderer. His every word was a snare, a tiny part of a giant net, which tangled Thoma Kunj slowly but consistently, step by step. In the eyes of others, Thomas Kunj had no escape, no exit, as his guiltlessness vanished like the morning mist over the mountain peak. Thoma Kunj did not show any attachment to his very existence. He was detached from what was happening in the court and was not concerned about what would happen. That expression was an acceptance of his guilt for the public prosecutor.

On some occasions, Thoma Kunj thought to accept the guilt. A poor girl was raped and murdered by someone, and someone had to own up to the crime. It was essential somebody said he did it, and there was no one getting up from the audience in the court and saying, "Yes, I did it." It was wrong not to accept the guilt as someone needed to have done it. But he thought it was his duty to confess the responsibility and stop the further trial. Never in life had Thoma Kunj been in such a quagmire that his mind asked him to own up to something he did not do. It was to help the judge not continue with a trial with no visible criminal. It had a victim, and it was inevitable there was a murderer; it was his duty to own it up even though he was not the offender. But he was the accused, even though he did not rape the girl, strangulate her and dump her in the well. It was a stray thought, but against his convictions and beliefs.

In his silence, Thoma Kunj appeared as the rapist of a minor girl, even though he had never seen her. He had to carry the burden of a crime on his shoulders.

To be silent was beyond the privilege against self-incrimination. It was a right not to speak even about one's innocence, not defending oneself, as everyone had a duty to protect everybody and was responsible for not accusing others by making false accusations. Why one should defend oneself was an unanswered question for Thoma Kunj; no one could give him an appropriate answer, not even the judge.

It was withholding information about guiltlessness, as a person shouldn't trumpet one's glory.

"I am my attorney, but I don't want to speak about myself, as I believe I need not protect myself. It is the duty of other individuals and society not to tell lies about me," Thoma Kunj said to the judge when the court began on the last day, and the judge laughed at his inanity. The judge considered Thoma Kunj's argument vapid, empty, shallow or foolhardy.

Thoma Kunj looked at the judge in disbelief as he expected the judge not to have taken his silence as evidence against him.

The public prosecutor laughed loudly, joining the judge. Thoma Kunj looked at the public prosecutor with scepticism and amusement. He thought the judge and the public prosecutor were ignorant of the yearning of human hearts to be upright in all actions and beliefs.

The expressions of the public prosecutor would be triumphant when the judge proclaimed the verdict that Thoma Kunj was guilty. He raped, strangulated, and dumped the body of a minor girl in the well of the women's hostel.

There was bewilderment on the face of Thoma Kunj when he heard the public prosecutor's expressions of joy, a pleasure germinating from an innocent's agony. The public prosecutor knew he was weaving falsehoods for his politician friend's benefit; when he became a minister, he would be made a judge.

Thoma Kunj looked at the public prosecutor and the judge with disdain and pity.

His efforts were futile to convince anyone that he had never touched a girl or woman other than his mother,

Emily, Parvathy, and Ambika. He was unsuccessful in proving he never thought of raping a girl or woman as he never had such a flawed sexual urge.

He had never thought of strangulating anyone as he did not ever get angry with anyone other than Appu.

But Appu was vicious. He tried to humiliate Thoma Kunj in public, and his target was Thoma Kunj's Mama. Emily was his pride, and anyone who wanted to say a bad word about her broke his heart. He could not accept it; the pain was beyond his imagination.

His ignorance of human behaviour made him maintain a silence that others considered an expression of his criminality. His trust in anybody he met made him vulnerable, and his quietness and goodness stood against him. He had no clarity in explaining incidents, unsuccessful in understanding the police, law and court concepts. His simple life stood against him as if he was an introvert, asocial, and an enemy of people. While listening to the public prosecutor, Thoma Kunj doubted his conviction that he was guiltless, and he thought he might have raped her, choked her, and tossed the body in a pit without seeing and touching the girl.

Even at the gallows, the silence overshadowed everything except for a few minutes before the district magistrate read the warrant.

No prisoner was allowed to witness the execution of a fellow convict. Thoma Kunj knew that the prison superintendent, two senior jailors, and a minimum of twelve guards, including ten constables and two head constables, would be at the gallows. No priest would be there as Thoma Kunj did not believe in God. The Superintendent could allow social scientists, psychologists, and psychiatrists engaged in studies on the behaviour of murderers and convicts to witness the execution.

The execution would be before sunrise, and all prisoners would be locked in their barracks and cells.

Thoma Kunj would be hooded as he would not be allowed to see the gallows.

The prison was a universe of its own, a world for those who lost their freedom. For society, the loss of independence was due to the misappropriation of liberty. But if there was no freedom in the first place, where could Thoma Kunj appropriate his autonomy? Self-determination was lost to gain it, and if there was no self, self-rule disappeared into the wasteland of existence.

Thoma Kunj lost forever when his final appeal was rejected.

"The convict is a dangerous sexual predator; he is a threat to the peaceful co-existence of individuals who respect and obey the law of the land; his plea for clemency cannot be entertained."

The one-sentence verdict was precise; it forced the prison authorities to oil the gallows, which had not been used for a long time, and directed the Superintendent to get a sturdy noose to hang Thoma Kunj.

But the meaning of the phrase 'dangerous sexual predator' was beyond his understanding. He tried to make it understandable for the whole week but failed.

No one in gaol could make him grasp the meaning of it. He could have asked her to explain it in simple terms if his Mama were alive. He had seen her drafting letters for her school headmaster, who could not speak or write English correctly. If Parvathy and George Mooken were there, he could have asked them. But they left for America the same afternoon Thoma Kunj went to the women's hostel to repair the leaking pipeline at the overhead tank.

It was also equally challenging for Thoma Kunj to understand the meaning of the words, a threat to the peaceful co-existence of individuals. Thoma Kunj never became a danger to anyone, except for hitting Appu, who called his mother a veshya. He was in a rage as Appu had tried to malign the character of Mama. It was painful; it hurt him beyond repair. Two of his teeth were fallen, and he coughed out blood. That was the only time Thoma Kunj was a threat to the peaceful co-existence of individuals. But no one realised the gravity of malice in Appu's words. He had no business calling Mama a prostitute.

But the school deleted Thoma Kunj from the roll and refused to give him a transfer certificate; he could not join another school. As it was the end of his studies, George Mooken met the headmaster pleading for a transfer certificate, and he returned disappointed.

Thoma Kunj went to the piggery. He was good at castrating the piglets; his knife was sharp, and it took only two minutes for Thoma Kunj to do his job. Within two days, the piglets became normal; they ate more and became fat and big. There were more demands for the meat of castrated hogs. But he could not forget his school as he wanted to study, become an engineer, and travel abroad like Parvathy and Mooken. But Thoma Kunj slept dreaming of his piglets and liked the piggy smell.

The rejection of his first appeal was also sharp and piercing:

"The law demands impartiality, justice and equality. After strangulating a minor, the defendant raped her and dumped the body in a well. He has a history of serious misconduct. Prayer for clemency rejected."

Thoma Kunj failed to understand the authenticity of the words used in the verdict. Never in his life had such incidents happened, and he couldn't remember raping a minor, had no history of misconduct and never even hugged a person except his mother. When he was young, Parvathy used to hug him, planting sweet kisses on his forehead. For Thoma Kunj, the incident and accusations in the verdict and rejection of his appeals were fake. He had not once had sex with a woman, and he was thirty-five and parading towards the gallows for rape and murder of a minor.

Suddenly the parade stopped; no footsteps; there was total silence. Everyone was sleeping within the prison walls except the superintendent, jailors, doctor, guards, and Thoma Kunj. They had taken three minutes to reach the spot; it would take two minutes to the gallows. The district magistrate read the warrant; the executioner would lead him to scaffolds, place him over the trap door, and rope him around his neck. He would come close to the condemned and whisper in his ear:

"Forgive me; I am doing my duty."

His duty was to hang an innocent man. But it was not his duty to verify whether the condemned was truly guilty; that was the judge's duty. Like many other judges in countless cases, the judge failed in his task.

The executioner's final act was to pull the lever of the gallows. Then the doctor would verify whether the hanged was dead, and he would sign the final certificate.

It would take less than ten minutes from the cell to the gallows.

Another ten minutes while dangling from the noose within the pit.

Social scientists, psychologists, criminologists, and psychiatrists would start their endless debates, and numerous journalists would join them. They would write learned articles and anchor discussions.

The Superintendent turned back:

"Cover his face," he ordered.

The senior jailor took out a black stitched cloth and placed it on Thoma Kunj's head, neatly covering his face. He would no longer see the sun, moon, stars, animals, birds, trees, creepers, his beloved Ayyankunnu, the peaks of Attayoli covered with monsoon clouds, the Barapuzha, elephants and tigers on its banks, coconut farms, the piggery, or humans, including Parvathy, George Mooken and Razak.

Covering the head and face of the condemned with a black cloth before the hanging was a ritual to protect the dignity of the hanged. The convict should not see the gallows; no one would see his facial expressions and emotional upheavals while dangling from the noose. Society was anxious about the self-esteem of the condemned, even though it had no qualms in denying his freedom by accusing him of rape and strangulation of a minor girl, which the witnesses knew was false. But they accused Thoma Kunj as he was easy prey. All witnesses benefitted from telling a fiction. The warden protected the grown-up son of a politician standing for elections in the state assembly, the ultimate seat of lawmakers in Kerala.

Thoma Kunj spent eleven years in prison. By that time, a young man had become the Minister of Education in the state and visited many schools and colleges as a guest of honour. He advised girls to protect themselves from conceivable rape and the sexual misdemeanour of marauders like Thoma Kunj, vividly recollecting the one week he hid in the hostel warden's bedroom after he raped the minor girl and dumped her body in the well. The virile young man had never heard of Razak, but Thoma Kunj was not Akeem, and he forgot to defend himself.

The High Court, Supreme Court, and the President rejected Thoma Kunj's appeals, and the procession started with Thoma Kunj, the most protected human in India, for ten minutes. Once, he was in the Republic Day parade, and on the last day of his life, wearing a black cowl, he marched towards the gallows without guilt, deprived of speech.

Chapter Four

THE BLACK CLOTH

When Emily hanged herself from a cross, she was almost nude. It seemed as if she was hugging the naked Jesus.

Emily made her rope from coconut husk; it took about a week to finish. Around three-thirty in the morning, she opened her son's door, went near his bed, and looked at him for a minute. She lived only for him for thirteen years and refused to abort him when he was growing within her womb. When Thoma Kunj was born, Emily was nineteen.

Thirty-two was a young age to die.

Emily died alone on a cross in front of the church.

It was a rainy night; Emily was walking from her home; the rope was in her left hand, and a plastic stool was in her right. In the pitch dark, she walked about five hundred meters; she knew the path thoroughly as she had walked through it a thousand times, every Sunday, feast days, all saints' days, and all souls' days for thirteen years.

A dim light from the church's steeples cast long shadows over the gigantic dark granite cross, and the metal statue of Jesus looked like a large lizard.

Emily was a regular churchgoer, and Thoma Kunj accompanied her as a toddler.

Kurien refused to go to church; he did not believe in God; he preferred pigs.

Kurien did not oppose Emily and Thoma Kunj going to church; he never imposed his beliefs on others. He loved his wife and son and lived for them. When his aunt insisted on a church marriage with Emily, he went with her to church.

George Mooken and Parvathy gave him a job, and he was grateful. Kurien had just completed his one-year certificate course in pig farming from a veterinary college and saw a small advertisement for a pig farm supervisor. He travelled up to Ayyankunnu and met Parvathy and Mooken; they liked him and appreciated his enthusiasm, systematic approach, hope, and commitment. He was only seventeen. Kurien built a small shack in the corner of George Mooken's land, and later Mooken gifted him half an acre of land around the hut when Emily and Thoma Kunj joined him.

He worked with them for seven years before bringing Emily and Thoma Kunj to Ayyankunnu. For the first time, Kurien took a three-day holiday and went to Kottayam to meet his father's sister, Mariam, his only living relative. She was a nurse in the UK for forty years, and when her husband, a doctor, died, she returned to the house she and her spouse constructed in Kottayam, leaving her children and their children in England.

Kurien lost his mother when he was very young, and his father, a clerk in the tax collector's office, did not marry again, turned to alcohol, lost everything and died on a street corner. Since he was ten, Kurien had worked in a cowshed, continued his studies, matriculated, and then took a one-year certificate course in pig farming.

On the second day with his father's sister, around seven in the evening, Kurien saw a young pregnant woman sitting alone in Jubilee Park, next to his aunt's house. He recognised she needed help. It was drizzling and getting dark; he went close to her. From his piggy sense, he smelt she was in her last stage of pregnancy and needed immediate assistance. The woman told him she had nowhere to go, and Kurien asked her to go with him to his aunt's house without thinking about anything. She could not walk; Kurien carried her in his arms.

Mariam did not waste any time. She took Emily inside, cleaned her with warm water, fed her nourishing food and massaged her legs and arms. The whole night she did not sleep and remained with the pregnant woman. Precisely at five past four on the following day, Emily gave birth. Kurien was there to assist his aunt through the night, and he was the first to touch the child as his experience at George Mooken's pigsty helped him a lot.

On the seventh day, Mariam took the infant to her parish church; Emily and Kurien followed her. They baptised the child; Mariam suggested Thomas as the babe's name in memory of St Thomas the Apostle, the founder of Christianity in Kerala. The priest recited prayers in Aramaic-Syriac and Malayalam.

Mariam arranged a party and invited the parish priest, the sexton, the altar boys, and her immediate neighbours for that evening.

Kurien extended his holidays for one more week, a total of ten days, and he planned to return to Malabar, leaving Emily and Thoma Kunj in the care of Mariam the next day. He told Emily he would be going back the ensuing day. Emily looked at him and wept silently.

"Do you want to come with me? I work in a piggery; I don't have anything except a hut built in the land of my employer," Kurien said.

"I love to go with you anywhere on earth; I need no wealth, but only love and someone to love," Emily replied.

"Are you sure?" Kurien wanted to get assurance from Emily.

"Certainly. I will live with you and die with you," Emily said.

Kurien and Emily told Mariam about their decision. Mariam took them to the church again after presenting a wedding dress to Emily, a suit to Kurien and two wedding rings. Before the priest, Emily and Kurien exchanged the vows, a promise of love and devotion they made to each other. After pronouncing the vows, they exchanged the wedding rings on the fourth finger of the left hand, believing the ring finger had a vein running directly to their hearts. Thereupon the priest declared Emily and Kurien husband and wife.

"I now pronounce you husband and wife."

Finally, the priest blessed them "in the name of the Father, and of the Son, and the Holy Ghost."

Mariam expressed her desire to adopt Thoma Kunj, as Emily and Kurien would not be victims of gossip and character assassination. She genuinely loved Thoma Kunj and was willing to look after him as her grandson, educating him to be a doctor, engineer, or an IAS officer.

Emily could not imagine a world without her son and husband.

Mariam wanted to have someone to love during her old age, as she was tired of her lonely life; nonetheless, she understood Emily's love for her son.

Emily held Thoma Kunj close to her heart when they took a train from Kottayam to Thalassery.

It was Emily's first journey to Malabar, and she liked Ayyankunnu. Parvathy and George Mooken received Emily, Thoma Kunj and Kurien with open hands and arranged a party for all their workers in their farmhouse to welcome Emily and the babe. Parvathy talked to Emily endlessly and expressed happiness at meeting her and having her as her neighbour and friend.

George Mooken and Parvathy gifted Emily, Thoma Kunj and Kurien half an acre of land around their shelter.

Kurien and Emily started their life in their tiny cabin, and Parvathy and George Mooken promised to help them financially to build a house. Emily told them she needed to work and did not expect direct financial help. But as she had not done a teacher's training diploma, she was not qualified to get a job as a primary school teacher and had not completed college, making her ineligible to get other jobs.

Emily was ready to do any job and expressed willingness to work in the cowshed or piggery, but Parvathy discouraged her.

Emily applied for a sweeper's job in the school belonging to their parish church. The salary came from the government, but she couldn't pay a hefty bribe to the bishop, who was the school manager. George Mooken told Emily there was a vacancy for a sweeper in a school run by the government, about two kilometres away from their house, and Emily applied for the job. Within three months, Emily got an appointment order from the education officer.

The vicar was unhappy with Emily when she accepted a job in the government school. She explained to the parish priest it was difficult for her to pay the inducement to the church. Nonetheless, there was no need to pay any fix in the government school, as the criterion for the appointment was her qualification.

When he was five, Thoma Kunj started attending the church-run school, which was only a five-minute walk from home. George Mooken donated ten thousand rupees to the vicar to get a seat in the school. Thoma Kunj was a bubbly child, good at studies and extracurricular activities. Like his mother, he could speak well in Malayalam and English; many teachers felt jealous of him.

Thoma Kunj enjoyed having a piggyback ride with his arms around Kurien's neck and legs around his waist. Kurien loved carrying him on his back whenever he had time. Emily often laughed loudly, watching the father and son riding.

The family travelled up to Kannur and Thalassery, spent long hours on the beach and played throwing balls on the sand every three months. They watched Malayalam and Hollywood movies in the evening, stayed in a hotel, and loved eating out.

Twice they travelled up to Kottayam and stayed with Mariam, and she never forgot to give a bag full of gifts, including clothes, to Thoma Kunj and Emily. But the sudden demise of Mariam brought an end to their trips to Kottayam.

Thoma Kunj loved both Kurien and Emily. Every evening he waited for his father to return after long work hours in the piggery. Twice a week, Kurien went with a driver to Bangalore, Mysore, and other distant places in Karnataka, as Kurien managed the distribution of pork in many restaurants and hotels there. He never forgot to get gifts for Thoma Kunj, especially books on science and technology.

Kurien was Thoma Kunj's best friend, and Emily was his sibling. He shared his desires and expectations with her, and Emily listened to him eagerly. After the sudden death of Kurien, Emily discussed with Thoma Kunj their family, financial situations, and plans. When he was twelve, Emily shared her background with him, which she kept an intimate secret. Emily respected Thoma Kunj and thought he would become a mature person who could understand complex human problems by twelve. Thoma Kunj stood with his mother in all her anxieties and worries.

Thoma Kunj loved the way Emily looked. She had a rare charm, and he thought his Mama was beautiful. He loved to comb her short hair, which looked dark and lovely.

Emily was an active member of the women's group in her neighbourhood. Women liked her ability to speak and express her ideas in clear language. She visited many houses and stood with women and girls to solve several of their problems, such as the alcoholism of their husbands and family violence, where mostly women were the victims.

Every Sunday afternoon, Emily took Thoma Kunj to a Home for the Aged in the town about twelve kilometres from their house. Emily had a two-wheeler, and she drove it effortlessly. The Home for the Aged had about sixty-five inmates, mostly widowed and rejected women. Most women were in the age group of sixty-five to eighty years. Numerous volunteers used to visit the home to do voluntary work. Emily cleaned and mopped the dining hall, sitting rooms, dormitories, and lavatories. Sometimes she washed the inmates' clothes in the washing machine, gave baths to the inmates, and dried their bodies with towels. Thoma Kunj was always with Emily, and he helped his mother with the work. He developed an affinity and love for older people and tried to understand their emotions, especially anguish, anxiety, sadness and sorrow. He knew widowed women were pushed out of their homes by their sons, and some had miserable life on street corners. Most windows were kept in institutions by their close relatives, primarily their children. Thoma Kunj listened to their stories with empathy. Those women faced quite a few problems: they outlived their husbands, children settled abroad, and some women gave up all their property to children, trusting they would look after them in their old age.

The closeness and kinship with those rejected influenced Thoma Kunj in developing his goal in life, self-detachment. He felt one with all inmates of the home; their stories were his story, their pain was his pain, their hope was his hope, and their joy was his joy. His perception of the purpose of human life resulted from the totality of his experiences with others, and it grew like a banyan tree, providing shade to everyone. He overcame his existence and embraced the feelings of others, developing an equal responsibility for the welfare of the other, as there was no difference between him and the other.

Thoma Kunj forgot himself; he evolved as the other.

Emily's inspiration in the emotional and psychological growth of Thoma Kunj was prominent in his words and actions. He grew up without a dominant ego that shaped his life and future. Emily was the centre of his attraction; her affection for others, simplicity, courage, and straightforwardness fascinated him.

Emily was elected a member of the local parish council as one of the representatives of women. Three women and seven male members belonged to the board. The other two women were nuns from the convents who were teachers in the parish school. The nuns always showed superiority as they were graduates and teachers. They treated Emily as an untouchable a woman without any status in society. They were jealous as Emily was a better speaker who could convey her ideas effectively. They were envious because Emily knew better English and had no fear; she openly expressed her opinions.

The priest discouraged women from speaking in the parish council meeting, and the nuns kept a profound silence. Whenever Emily wanted to talk, the vicar reminded her that the meeting was for men and the women's job was to listen to the vicar. Emily expressed her disagreement with the priest, and gradually it became customary for the vicar to ridicule Emily that she had not read the Bible to know the position of women in the church. Most men agreed with the priest and chastised Emily for her assertive behaviour. They said a woman should not be bold before the parish priest.

The priest took the Bible and read St Paul's first letter to Timothy:

"I do not permit a woman to teach or assume authority over a man; she must be quiet."

After reading the passage, the priest said women had only a subordinate position in the church and society. They needed to obey men, especially the parish priest.

Emily did not say anything. She kept a thoughtful silence.

On another occasion, Emily wanted to speak about girls in the parish who were denied college education, as many parents preferred higher education to their sons. The priest asked her to shut her mouth, telling her she should have remained silent in her family and church. She was not allowed to speak but must be in submission.

Emily told the priest he was still in the Middle Ages; the world had changed drastically for centuries, and women had achieved name and fame. Besides, no culture or civilisation could survive without women's participation.

The parish priest gestured violently and shouted at Emily. The two nuns and almost all men supported the vicar in abusing Emily. But Emily told the priest he was the worst misogynist she had ever seen. The priest was raging and removed Emily from the parish council. In the next meeting, another nun was elected to the committee.

It did not affect Emily, and she discussed everything with Kurien, who told her they could live without church and God. Even though both had a substantial influence on human life, it was easy to live without them if they decided to reject them. Consider religion and God as mythical and superstitious, oppressive and patriarchal, vicious offshoots of the evolutionary process of culture. Males created religion for males to oppress women and keep them in slavery and sexual misappropriation. History highlights males used religion as a weapon to suppress sane voices, social progress and democracy. Religion was always against democracy and enlightenment. Emily listened to Kurien with interest, as her husband understood the yearning of women searching for freedom and equality, especially his wife. He stood with her like a rock in her tribulations.

Emily and Kurien loved and cherished each other's company, and Thoma Kunj learned basic lessons of affection from them. Their presence was enriching to him, and he observed them minutely in their words and actions. They were always an inspiration for him.

Following his mother and father, Thoma Kunj developed a philosophy of life beyond egoism. Everyone had a place to exist with dignity as he loved to share gifts from his parents, George Mooken and Parvathy, with other students in his school. From childhood, he understood others too, had pains and sorrows, anxiety and sadness, and they could negatively affect everyone's lives, and he had a duty to help them cherish their life. He refused to tell lies and abstained from causing pain to others. Other students had the same desire he had, similar feelings he kept in his heart, and similar worries he carried within himself. He noticed almost all boys and girls behaved with compassion and consideration until the fourth grade. Once they entered the fifth grade or reached ten years of age, they steadily lost empathy and equanimity. There was a desire in Thoma Kunj to remain as he was, practising what he learned from his parents and the values they inculcated in him. But it created strain and conflicts in his life, as others watched him with doubt, made mischievous comments about him and sometimes made him the victim of spiteful plans.

When he travelled with his parents or alone, he was civil with his fellow passengers; sometimes, his behaviour was misinterpreted. He learned he shouldn't be too friendly with others, especially strangers. Thoma Kunj had his first flight from Calicut airport to Kochi, and he was aghast to see passengers pushing and elbowing each other towards the aircraft entrance. The same behaviour was noticed during deplaning, which he witnessed in big towns and marketplaces. Basic human behaviour was the same in all situations and could not be changed, as humans conducted themselves like animals during extreme conditions. There was no difference between the actions of the highly educated, powerful, wealthy, influential, and the illiterate, frail, poor and noninfluential, Thoma Kunj learned when he read the story of the plane crash victims on the Andes. Some passengers survived till the search parties arrived, resorting to cannibalism.

Thoma Kunj could not agree with those who supported the position of Captain Dudley of Mignonette, who, along with his two sailors, killed and ate Richard Parker, the cabin boy. They were shipwrecked in the South Atlantic and had no food for nineteen days. Killing and eating the cabin boy was their only option. Thoma Kunj reflected on the nature of laws governing people's collective life. He developed a value system that specific duties and rights should command society's respect for reasons independent of social consequences. People were biologically self-centred and behaved for their benefit, like any other animal, but Thoma Kunj wanted to be different; he wanted to live unselfishly, respecting the feelings of others.

Thoma Kunj became lonely and silent, confronting wrongdoing everywhere, especially in school. His friends became more and more self-conscious, interested in self-growth, and consequently, demeaning others. Most teachers encouraged individuality and personal achievement; it pained Thoma Kunj. When he was selected to participate in the Republic Day parade, almost all his friends gossiped against him instead of praising and encouraging him. Suddenly, he became their target of envy, but for Thoma Kunj, he had never taken away anything from them, spoken any ill against them or hurt them.

He saw a big divide between him and his friends, which was difficult to bridge.

"He is a sweeper's son, and how could they select him?" some asked. For them, the criterion for selection was the parents' status, social background, and financial conditions.

"His dead father worked in a piggery, and he participates in the Republic Day parade," a few teachers also commented.

Thoma Kunj felt pity for his teachers. Their vision of humanity was slender, parochial, disparaging value systems, and void of self-respect.

The standard for measuring human ability and humanness was different. The teachers and students did not see it as a collective achievement, a common cause for celebration and happiness. Instead, they infused hatred and jealousy. Thoma Kunj did not take away anything given to someone else; his selection to participate in the Republic Day Parade was based on clear, specific and confident choices, and he met those measures. Still, Thoma Kunj did not believe he was more meritorious, as merit should not have been a principle in selection because it was an outcome of a particular social and psychological background that others might not have received. So, the effort was not a reason for merit.

But Thoma Kunj experienced rejection from his friends due to his background and merit; both were not his creation, and he wanted to denounce both. His life was an experiment to be different; he craved a different perception of life and observed events through an unselfish prism of life. No one taught him to do so, but it was enlightenment, a new awareness, and the focus was not to hurt anyone. He did not want to tell a lie or defend himself and desired to keep silent. The loss of his father shaped him in that new process of evolution. He put himself in others' shoes, and others failed to see him as a selfless man, or they failed to be unselfish and not self-centred.

It was a struggle for Thoma Kunj, like Emily's fight with the parish priest. It was painful and hard to forget as self-needed constant training. He observed others, learned that each individual had a goal in life, and strived to achieve it. Everyone had sad and happy backgrounds; they were as painful or precious as his own.

Working with his mother, Emily, in the Home for the Aged was a metanoia; it changed his mind, heart, and way of life. He started seeing others in him and himself in others. But once he got angry with a fellow being, that changed his life drastically. He never intended to hit Appu; nonetheless, it happened. It had painful penalties. Striving his best to have a peaceful co-existence was not enough; enemies could emerge from nowhere. It happened to Emily too.

The vicar disliked Emily raising questions in the parish council meeting. Even though he removed her from the council's membership, he held a grudge against her in his mind. Whenever there was an opportunity, he tried to humiliate Emily publicly. But Emily could speak logically and humbly, exposing the priest's arrogance and ignorance. The vicar thought of embarrassing her in his Sunday homily when she would not get an opportunity to talk. The vicar knew Emily was regular in Sunday services and planned to chasten Emily during his sermon. His Sunday talks were mainly from the gospels and the apostles' epistles, and for many Sundays, he searched for a quote from St. Paul.

That Sunday, the reading was from first Corinthians chapter eleven, and his sermon was on that reading. In a clear voice, he repeated what he had read.

"A man is the glory of God, and for this reason, he ought not to have his head covered. A woman is the glory of man." Then he looked at the believers assembled in the church, and his eyes searched for Emily like a fierce bald eagle hunting for a rabbit. She was sitting on the second row of pews; she never covered her head in the church, exposing her short hair.

As if to the devotees, he continued his sermon, "a woman should cover her head."

Emily was the only woman who refused to cover her head in the church, and she understood that the priest was talking about her. Women and men looked at Emily with vicious curiosity, and some started gossiping. The priest felt happy that Emily and the congregation understood the deeper meaning of what he said.

Once again, looking at Emily, the priest said:

"It is disgraceful for a wife to cut off her hair."

After a few seconds of silence, the priest spoke again:

"If the husband lacks grace, what the wife does is his glory."

The priest was targeting her dead husband. Kurien was not a believer, and he never attended the service in a church. It was irreligious for a priest to speak ill of a person who was no more, that too standing on the pulpit. An evil act had no edge, and a vicar could become very nasty once he got unrestricted power, and the audience could not react and were prohibited from countering. Kurien had a golden heart and was a nobleman opposite the priest. Emily's heart burned, and her blood boiled. But she was restricted from reacting by society, as the church was a consecrated place, where the priest transubstantiated bread and wine into the body and blood of Christ for the remembrance of the last supper and the crucifixion. The priest should not have spoken evil against a dead man and his wife's physical appearance. Hairdo was a woman's personal choice, an expression of her freedom and equality; no priest, no church had the power to deny it, to speak ill about it.

Kurien had no objection to Emily trimming her hair; he was happy to see her hairstyle and always encouraged her to be a free woman according to her needs and selections. While looking at the priest, Emily wanted to roar, "shut your foul mouth, don't speak ill of women," but she controlled herself. In the first century, a madman from Tarsus, a Greek fanatic and a male chauvinist, wrote idiotic letters to the males of Corinth. He wanted to control the progressive women who were always one step ahead of their husbands. His name was Paul, and he claimed to be a disciple of Jesus even though he had never met Jesus. But Paul transformed Jesus into Christ, an imaginary being, an amalgamation of man and God, a sexless son of God.

Paul was a joker, an oppressor, a fundamentalist who had the experience of subjugating women friends of Jesus, who always walked with Jesus and listened to his parables. They were with him when he was betrayed by a male disciple, Judas Iscariot. Another male, Peter, ran away from Jesus once Jesus was taken to Golgotha. When the Romans crucified him, his women friends were with him; all the men, except John, disappeared and hid in darkness to save themselves. Mary Magdalene spent three nights at his grave, and when he was resurrected, she was the first person to see him. She was stupefied with joy and happiness and called him "my Lord," a term used in Hebrew and Aramaic for husband.

The male disciples of Jesus wanted to deny Mary Magdalene, her husband. They tried to rob her, her position, and her intimacy and called her a prostitute. The male disciples of Jesus denied women their rightful position in the church. And Emily thought the priest was doing the same. Even after twenty centuries, the church continued to live in that denial. It wanted to be an organisation of misogynists. Emily got up from her seat; she looked around; the whole congregation looked at her.

"I am ashamed of the vicar. His words are not of Jesus; he misuses the pulpit to speak ill about a widow; I object to his demeaning words about my late husband. Even though he was an atheist, he never harmed anyone or spoke ill of others. If the cleric believes in God, he is answerable to Him," Emily said calmly and walked out.

There was pin-drop silence within the church. The congregation looked at the priest in disbelief, and no one could understand what the preacher said in his remaining homily.

The Sunday sermon created unending arguments, tensions and conflicts among the parishioners that continued for many months. It divided the faithful into three clear groups, those who supported the priest, the most significant majority. They were afraid of the priest and bishop, fearful of the priest's curse, refusal of baptism, marriage ceremonies, and burial within the church cemetery. To have jobs in church-run schools, colleges, hospitals and other institutions, even though the parishioners had to pay bribes, they needed the support and recommendation of the priests and bishop. Some took a neutral position. Abusing a woman during the sermon was not an issue; they were self-centred. A small minority strongly objected to the abusive language of the priest during his Sunday talk. They were not explicitly supporting Emily but objecting to the priest's wanton words against a woman and her dead husband. There were only half a dozen such parishioners, and they were very vocal.

After six months, Emily received a message from the bishop that he wished to see her in the bishopric in the town. After the death of Kurien, Emily did not once travel to the town; there was no one to go with her. She did not want to take a day's leave from school or ask Thoma Kunj to miss his class by going with her. After a month, the bishop intimated his displeasure to Emily through the parish priest. He sent a letter to the priest to be read during a Sunday sermon. In his letter, the bishop firmly said no parishioner should speak within the church without the vicar's permission. Arguing with the priest or raising counterquestions during or after the homily was not acceptable, and if anyone dared to do so, that person might face ex-communication. The bishop's message was a solid and severe warning to the faithful. He conveniently kept silent about the misdemeanour of the parish priest in abusing Emily during his Sunday speech.

The bishop's letter gave the vicar new vigour, a license to abuse anyone, even during the Sunday service.

He rejoiced in his freedom and power and craved an opportunity to test it on Emily. He knew not many supported the widow openly, fearing gossip. The priest rehearsed his speech many times, mainly in the bathroom. Emily's face appeared before him repeatedly as hidden appreciation for her looks, and personal courage filled his heart. He consciously initiated sexual fantasies about her, hugging and making love. But he often felt dejected by his failure to fulfil his urges, and Emily remained a target of his mental abuse. The priest's incubated erotic desires overwhelmed him, which tossed him into a hell of distress, frustration, and hatred. Each time he approached the pulpit, his eyes combed the congregation for Emily.

Emily did not attend church for many weeks; her objection was listening to a hate-monger. It was a Sunday, the second death anniversary of Kurien, and Emily thought of going to the church; and as usual, the church was filled with believers. Emily was the only woman who did not cover her head; her decision was based on the refusal of imposed values, a rebellion against Paul's teachings, and forcing women to be slaves of men. It was also a revolt against the church, the bishop and the priests who preached to oppress women and use them as mere sexual objects.

The second reading was from the Gospel of John: "I am the world's light. Whoever follows me never walks in darkness but will have the light of life." The priest then started the sermon based on the first reading from Paul's epistle, ignoring the Gospel: "Your body is not meant for sexual immorality, but for the Lord, and the Lord for the body."

The priest paused for a minute and looked at the congregation, probing specific faces. He saw Emily in the middle row; she listened attentively to his words. Then he read another quote from Paul: "Everyone who joins himself to a prostitute becomes one with her body." Emily thought of the irrelevance of the passage in that particular context as the gospel reading was about Jesus as the light and following him in his light. Whereas the sermon was on prostitution.

There was a long pause, and the priest again looked at Emily. Then in a loud voice, he said: "We refuse to be with a prostitute among us." The believers felt stunned, and they looked at each other.

"Your body is a temple of the Holy Spirit. Honour God with your body," he said, looking at the parishioners and verifying the range of emotions on their faces. "My dear people, there is a veshya among us. She is a black mark on our parish. No veshya should be with us." The preacher emphasised the Malayalam word 'veshya' for a prostitute.

"I command the veshya to leave the church," the priest thundered, looking at Emily.

Emily felt a shiver in her body. The priest accused Emily of sexual transgression and humiliated her in front of parishioners within the church during a Sunday mass.

"I am not a veshya; you are falsely accusing me," Emily got up from her seat and roared. Her voice echoed within the church walls, and the congregation looked at her in disbelief.

Then Emily walked out of the church. She did not cry, but her heart was bursting. Before the gigantic cross in front of the church, like a lonely prehistoric Stonehenge, Emily looked at the victim's naked body for a minute.

"Only you and I are not inside the church," she murmured.

Jesus kept silent.

"Why should we be inside, in a hell of hatred and humiliation?" she asked the crucified saviour.

"It is better to be here, Emily, hanging," she heard as if Jesus was inviting her.

"It is better to be with you, embracing you," she said as she walked away.

The road was empty.

Thoma Kunj was preparing to attend church for his catechism and the faith formation classes for Catholic children. In the catechism classes, the main lessons were on the New Testament, the story about the trinity, the birth and death of Jesus, the church, the creed, prayers, sacraments, and morality. The vicar had the final say in the catechism class.

"Why did Mama come back so early?" he wondered.

"Mama, what happened to you? Are you not well?" He asked.

"Nothing," she said and went inside.

Emily was a changed person; she lost interest in life. She took leave from school for two weeks, which was unusual. It looked as if she was trying to solve a riddle that had no solution, as she could not digest the insult within the church during a sermon when almost all parishioners were present. The preacher called her a veshya, the most disgraceful word in any language, a character assassination, a cruel joke. The priest questioned the personality, conduct and dignity of a widow, a mother, and a church member. Emily wanted to cry for days together; as crying would help her, it would wash away the hatred expressed by a priest, an opportunity to burst sorrows and hurts like a volcano. She repeatedly tried to weep, shout and yell, craving to tell the vicar what he did was wrong against the spirit of Jesus expressed throughout his life.

Low self-esteem oppressed Emily and brought feelings of rejection as if no one wanted her. It was a feeling of worthlessness, of a stray dog wandering the street corners for pity. Her mind travelled aimlessly like a vagabond, without purpose in life, an aimless traversing. She felt like vomiting frequently and could not eat or drink; disgust and anguish engulfed her inner self. Opening her eyes widely, probing awful situations as if she wanted to crush them, throw them entirely into unfathomable gorges, she looked at the void.

It was an affront for her, abusing her very existence, person, feelings, desires, hope, family, and life. The anxiety that emerged from that insult injured her mind and heart. She refused to talk even to Thoma Kunj, who pleaded with her to tell him what happened to her. Thoma Kunj hugged his Mama and told her he loved her, cared for her, and lived only for her. Emily looked at her son in silence for a long time. But she looked blank.

"Mon, I can't go on anymore," she said.

"Tell me what happened to you?" he asked.

"The vicar insulted me during his sermon," she replied.

"Mama, I am with you; I will ask him to apologise," he tried to console her.

"He called me a veshya in front of the whole congregation. It destroyed my self-esteem, my dignity as a human," Emily said.

"Mama, I will confront the vicar and compel him to apologise. He must visit you here in our house and beg your pardon. I will see; he will do it," Thoma Kunj said.

"I don't want to see his face," she replied.

"Then I will ask him to express his regret to the congregation on a Sunday," he insisted.

Thoma Kunj ran towards the church.

The priest briskly walked on the ground near his residence in the evening sun with another priest. Thoma Kunj gathered all his courage and told the priest that insulting his mother during his Sunday sermon was wrong and that he should express his regret to the congregation during the Sunday service. The priest laughed at him and told him his mother was a veshya, as Thoma Kunj was born before her marriage to Kurien. Thoma Kunj told him that what he said was abusive, character assassination of a woman. It was none of his business to read his mother's history before the parishioners. Besides, his mother had told him about his birth. The priest angrily reminded Thoma Kunj that he was born out of sin. Thoma Kunj looked at the priest for a minute and asked him to read the Gospel about the birth of Jesus, as he was also born without a father; Mary was single. Hearing Thoma Kunj, the priest was in a rage and shouted at him, retelling that the birth of Jesus was a mystery, a gift of God to humanity. Jesus was the son of God and was born through the Holy Spirit. Mary remained a virgin before and after the birth of Jesus.

"That is your belief, not mine," replied Thoma Kunj.

"*Poda patti*," the priest yelled at Thoma Kunj.

Thoma Kunj was a curse, and God would punish him for the unforgivable blasphemy, the priest continued to scream.

Thoma Kunj ran to George Mooken and told him what had happened to his mother and about his confrontation with the vicar. George Mooken said he and Parvathy did not go to church on the previous Sunday as both were in Bangalore with their daughter Anupama.

George Mooken immediately met the priest and told him his actions were wrong and that he needed to apologise. He recapped the Sermon on the Mount to the priest to learn from Jesus. The priest laughed at George Mooken and told him to mind his business. Mooken reminded the cleric that love and compassion were the core values of the Christian life, but he lacked them.

Parvathy and George Mooken went to see Emily. Parvathy hugged her friend telling her she was away with her daughter for a week and did not know Emily's tribulations. She assured Emily she would be with her and support her, as she considered Emily, her best friend.

Parvathy visited Emily daily and spent long hours with her, providing her emotional and psychological support and care. Parvathy noticed consistent social withdrawal in Emily's activities. She had inhibitions about talking to others and was afraid to share her worries.

Thoma Kunj observed persistent mood changes in Emily, besides being disinterested in managing personal hygiene and appearance. The uncharacteristically reckless behaviour of his mother, poor diet, rapid weight loss and lengthy silences worried him. Swift mood changes, signs of sadness, anxiety, anger, and self-pity were prominent in his mother. Her appearance was pathetic, as her eyelids dropped considerably, muscles became flaccid, head hanging, lips lowered, cheeks and jaws sank downwards, and the chest contracted.

Emily's mouth corners dipped downward, and she remained motionless and passive for many days. Thoma Kunj discussed the problem with Parvathy, and she suggested Emily might require psychotherapy to regain her old self to overcome the deep feelings of insult. With Thoma Kunj's consent, Parvathy wanted to take Emily to Bangalore for psychotherapy for a month.

Emily was quiet for many days and busy husking coconuts. Thoma Kunj wondered why his mother was unusually silent. He realised something was burning within her, but he failed to fathom the volcano's enormity. Thoma Kunj sat by his mother's side and coaxed her into speaking. Emily looked at him, and her eyes were dry; they had lost their brightness, lustre, radiance, and opalescence.

Parvathy made arrangements to go to Bangalore with Emily the following Sunday. She had contacted a group of psychotherapists in a counselling centre to help Emily regain her usual composure and personality; thereby, she could concentrate and increase her willpower to face and eliminate emotional, psychological and social problems. The goal was to strengthen the mind and enlarge her consciousness to enable Emily to use her full mental potential, bringing emotional contentment and social well-being. Parvathy would stay with Emily throughout the session until she completely recovered from her problem.

It was raining early in the morning. As usual, the sexton reached the church to ring the bell at six and prepare for the Sunday service; the bell tower was on the right side of the church. He saw a long white cloth hanging from the cross. He thought a white curtain cloth from the steeples might have fallen in the wind. The crack of the dawn was still draped with dark patches, and he went under the foot of the cross and looked up.

"Jesus," he gasped.

It was a woman hanging from the cross hugging the naked Jesus. Her white saree had fallen off, her blouse was torn, her shoulders exposed, and she was almost nude.

The sexton ran to the bell tower and rang the bell nonstop. The first who reached there were nuns from the nearby convents. People from the neighbourhood ran towards the church to see what had happened, and within ten minutes, there was a large crowd. Then the vicar appeared.

Someone ran towards the police station, and others called the police on their mobile phones.

A deep silence permeated the crowd for some time. Nobody could believe their eyes. Then gradually, whispering, gossiping and loud talking started. There was a curiosity to find out who the person was, her name.

Soon the police van appeared, lights flashing. The officer directed his constables to lower the dead body from the cross. The cops used a ladder to climb up. Thoma Kunj watched them with anxiety as he could not locate Mama when he got up. He had looked for her all over the house. While running towards the church, he searched for her on the road. The saree over the cross looked like his mother's. Parvathy put her arms around Thoma Kunj while standing near him.

The cops lowered the corpse and placed it on the platform on which the cross stood.

"It's Emily," shouted someone in the crowd.

"Emily, Emily, Emily," the name spread like wildfire.

Thoma Kunj collapsed. George Mooken carried him and placed him in his car.

After the autopsy, the body was returned on the third day. As Thoma Kunj was only fourteen, George Mooken signed the papers at the coroner's office and the police station. The vicar refused to allot a grave to the dead in the cemetery, quoting the rule book that a suicide victim's body could not be buried in a holy place.

"She was a sinner; her sins doubled by killing herself," the vicar said to George Mooken.

George Mooken pleaded with the priest to show mercy to a widow who was no more. The vicar asked him to meet him in his chamber, and Mooken understood the meaning of his words. He returned home, took five bundles of thousand-rupee notes, and met the priest in his room. Before six in the evening, the priest allowed George Mooken to bury Emily in the Themmadi Kuzhi, a corner section in the cemetery where sinners were buried.

Thoma Kunj, Parvathy, George Mooken and some farmworkers were present for the burial. No prayers were offered for the dead. The sexton supervised the funeral. The body was in a black coffin. After kissing his mother's forehead, Thoma Kunj covered his Mama's body with a black cloth. Parvathy placed a bundle of roses, lilies, and jasmine flowers over the black fabric and wept silently.

Thoma Kunj refused to cry, but he was silent. Parvathy and George Mooken requested him to sleep in their house. Parvathy was ready to adopt him as her son; however, Thoma Kunj insisted he goes home, lives alone, and cook his food at home. On the next day, he bundled all pictures of the Sacred Heart of Jesus, the Virgin Mary, all saints, rosaries and crosses of different sizes and shapes Emily had gathered over the years and burned them in his courtyard. He picked the ash in a plastic bag and threw it in the urine pit attached to the pigsty.

Thoma Kunj became an orphan when he was fourteen. His father died three years ago, but his mother cared for him and loved him as if nothing had happened.

Kurian was a loving father; Thoma Kunj always loved his company. After the death of Kurien, Emily had financial problems; the salary she was getting from the school as a sweeper was insufficient to run a family. The compensation George Mooken and Parvathy paid for the death of Kurien she deposited in a bank in the name of Thoma Kunj for his studies.

When Kurien was alive, Emily rejoiced in her son's daily presence. Kurien called him Thoma, and Emily, Kunj Mon. In school, he was Thomas Emily Kurien. She played with him, danced with him, sang songs and told him stories of yonder years, keeping everything to herself till he was twelve.

His primary school was about a five-minute walk; Thoma Kunj was confident enough to go alone. She taught him the alphabet of Malayalam and English, and he learned both languages rather effortlessly.

Emily noticed her son was talkative as a toddler; he had many friends in the school for the first four years. He played with them and celebrated their childhood. Thoma Kunj told them stories that Mama narrated at bedtime. He was always in a group of friends; they walked, played, studied and ate together.

Then his friends started gossiping about him, and it pained him. He gradually started withdrawing from students, teachers, and others who spoke ill of him. He told his Mama everything that happened in the school, and she consoled him and asked him to forget everything, as they were jealous.

"Wear glasses for seeing what is good," Mama said once.

And Thoma Kunj wore a mental glass, covering his eyes to see the good only; he forgot to speak ill about anyone and refused to hurt anyone or defend himself. When Mama died, Thoma Kunj turned defenceless.

On the way to the gallows, the jailor covered Thoma Kunj with a mask over his head. It was a black mask, as dark as night. He became blind and marched towards the gallows, not knowing the country had already hanged seven hundred and fifty-two condemned prisoners since independence. A few dozen more might not affect the consciousness of Hammurabi and Bentham's children. The political elites and the bureaucrats needed the noose to frighten the voiceless, the illiterate, and the rejected. The loop around the neck of Thoma Kunj protected the young education minister.

Suddenly he was at the gallows, and Thoma Kunj sensed a small crowd, a selected few including the district magistrate, researchers, and prison personnel. He could not see them because he was not allowed to see them, prohibited from visiting the gallows with a hanging noose. Mama could not see anybody because she was covered with a black cloth before her burial. She had been in the grave for twenty-two years when Thoma Kunj was taken to the gallows after eleven years in prison.

Chapter Five

THE GALLOWS

The gallows stood like twin headless palm trees connected by a crossbar. Thoma Kunj sensed its formidable proximity, and in pitch darkness, he could distinguish where it hoisted, how big it was, and how he would stand in the middle of its pillars to get the noose around his neck. It was a ceremony, like the circumcision of Adil, the castration of Razak, the raping of a minor girl in a government women's hostel or the crucifixion of Jesus.

The gallows negated freedom, and Thoma Kunj had no escape from non-freedom, as it was inevitable. No exit from the scaffold ever existed, like self-determination from birth, escape from death, and autonomy from millions of other events between birth and death. Life took place in a giant wheel of determinism, like a football game on a vast playground where one had no freedom to break the guidelines. One who played beyond the rules was kicked out beyond the boundary.

Imprisonment was the antithesis of freedom; one had no choice in it. Captivity was like angst over lost virginity. There was no freedom in rape, no liberation from death.

Death was the ultimate defeat. Thoma Kunj could not resist death; bereavement would be the final victor.

Incarceration was like the shadow of one's persona—pernicious, perilous, recurrent, and debilitating.

Even the monsoon in Malabar was not free; it couldn't come and go as it wished. There was thunder and lightning, rain and flood, and it seemed the earth celebrated its freedom to decide.

Even the gallows had no freedom.

Freedom was a myth; his parents created Thoma Kunj for pleasure. His biological father did not ask him when he decided to abort him. His mother had no freedom to save him; she did not know how to protect him or where to go for the delivery. Kurien carried her to his aunt's place, and Mariam had no freedom to reject Emily as a nurse's job was not to discard; she loved humanity. Life was a fable for Thoma Kunj; the Karnataka police did not ask Kurien's permission to thrash him before killing him violently like a wild boar. Thoma Kunj lost his father, who loved him like his son, even though he was not his father. Razak wanted Thoma Kunj to spend his life with him in Ponnani, but Thoma Kunj had no freedom to go to Ponnani and reject the gallows. Razak wanted a son, but Akeem castrated him to protect his houris in his Mashrabiya. Razak, a Muslim, abandoned Allah and wished to adopt Thoma Kunj, a Catholic who rejected the corrupt Church, burned the pictures of his God and buried the ash in the urine pit of pigs.

Emily did not ask Thoma Kunj's approval to hang herself on a cross, hugging the naked Jesus; Emily had no choice in dangling herself; the vicar forced it on her, calling her a prostitute. But she had the independence to select a cross or a tree branch. Thoma Kunj had to discontinue his studies as he hit Appu in the face for calling his mother a prostitute. Appu might have heard from his friends that the parish priest called Emily a veshya in his Sunday homely. The vicar was assured he had complete freedom to poke anyone during his sermon. When dismissed from school, Thoma Kunj could not go to another school. After the death of Emily, he had to work for a living, even though George Mooken and Parvathy were ready to adopt him as their son. But Thoma Kunj chose not to depend on anyone, as he had no internal freedom to say yes to their invite. He preferred the pigsty as he liked the odour his father Kurien brought home every evening, and Thoma Kunj loved the piggy smell of Kurien, whom he called Papa.

After the death of Kurien and Emily, Thoma Kunj decided to live a lonely life, and his privilege was to castrate the pigs on the pig farm of George Mooken. Thoma Kunj had no freedom to say no to George Mooken, refusing to go to the hostel to repair the leaking pipeline. George Mooken had no space to say no to the hostel warden, and the hostel warden had no liberty to tell the MLA she would not save his son from rape and murder charges, as he was a powerful man who could take an adverse decision against her. His son was a young man who would be a successful politician and a minister in the state one day. The hostel warden trapped Thoma Kunj; the MLA was happy, and his son was jubilant, even though they all carried the burden of guilt. Within ten years, the son became a minister who visited girls' schools and colleges, advising students to protect themselves from sexual predators.

Thoma Kunj had no liberty to defend himself, as he believed self-defence was not essential to live a peaceful life. He felt everyone needed to protect everyone in society, and somebody had to accept the guilt of raping and killing the minor girl. Thoma Kunj was silent as he knew he did not commit a crime. Like a rabbit accused of eating a tiger cub, he was charged with raping a minor girl and murdering her but did not know a hyena had eaten the tiger cub. Thoma Kunj kept silent like Emily, Razak, and the pigs in George Mooken's abattoir. Even though he never guillotined a pig, he could feel its pain, sorrows, and tears, and sometimes, he thought of guillotining himself to save the pigs. He castrated the pigs and was sorry for it, and each time before the castration, he asked for its pardon like an executioner asking for the condemned convict's forgiveness. Thoma Kunj remained silent when he castrated the pigs, but Adil cried aloud when Akeem castrated Razak. The concubines in the Mashrabiya blubbered when Akeem searched for Razak, holding the Egyptian's head in one hand and the sword in the other. Those women of the harem wept for Razak, not for their co-concubine.

Akeem had no freedom as he had to run his harem. He became a slave of his sexual pleasures and needed to maintain his laws within the seraglio. Razak's Padachon created the houris, seventy-two, for a faithful believer in paradise as a reward for fighting against his enemies, slicing their heads. The houris fulfilled Khuda's promise to give hope and courage to the sex-starved faithful believers, inspiring them to raid in the darkness of night the tiny communities of children of the one who wrestled with God the whole night scattered throughout the oasis of the desert. The sword fighters would have received the houris in paradise as repayment if they had died during the quick skirmishes that the sleeping men never expected. Seventy-two houris were a charming compensation for one's own lost life. If they were successful, the widows and the looted riches would have become their prize, and when they reached paradise, the houris.

The Merciful never thought about the liberty of the houris, as helpless women were condemned to be concubines on earth and houris in paradise.

Thoma Kunj did not worry about his bondage in his eleven years in prison; he accepted it as someone had to undergo imprisonment and possible execution for the rape and murder of a minor girl. He thought about the gallows but had no opportunity to see them; a fated prisoner was not given any work where the gallows stood. But Thoma Kunj had once overheard life-term prisoners describing the gallows as a massive death beam attached to two colossal elevated upright poles. The scaffold had no say in hanging a condemned prisoner; it was its duty, as the duty of houris, to provide sexual pleasure to the faithful believer in paradise.

Since the prison's inception, a scaffold made out of teak wood was used, and scores were hung on that. In the initial years of free India, hanging was the most straightforward means to eliminate a criminal; it was a free-for-all game. Migrating low-income families from Travancore to Malabar in search of land to cultivate, eliminate hunger and poverty, educate their children, and establish schools, churches, hospitals, and community centres created interminable conflicts with nature and people. The death penalty increased, hanging became common, and many innocents lost their lives on the gallows. No one was there to write their stories, and no one was interested in a dead man. The teak wood gallows were as strong as the Valapattanam bridge, and the noose tied around a condemned convict's neck was specially ordered from Coimbatore, the Manchester of India. A few years ago, a steel frame structure was erected by a steel factory known for its quality. The gallows protected the wealthy and powerful, the politicians, judges and ministers, priests, pandits, maulvis and businesspeople.

During the British era, there was no mercy for the criminal. Hundreds of semi-educated ruffians from Scotland, Wales, England and Ireland joined the British administrative service, especially in police and prison, encouraging ruthless suppression of lawbreaking. They wanted a mighty British empire to warm their hearth during the extreme winter. Each hanging pushed the share value of the East India Company to climb smoothly. For the British, the central philosophy of the criminal justice system included deterrence and retribution. The lawyers and judges who learned the Anglo-Saxon legal system quickly became the disciples of Hammurabi and Jeremy Bentham, showing a remarkable appetite for hanging. Many thousands were hanged since Maharaja Nandakumar's execution, an East India Company tax collector in Bengal. Free India gladly followed British brutality. Rasha Raghuraj Singh, executed on the ninth of September, the year the country got its independence at Jabalpur Central Prison, was the first to be hanged in free India.

Thoma Kunj walked to the gallows that stood like the sanctum sanctorum, the noose its deity, protected within high walls in the middle of a one-acre land, tiled with granite within a one-hundred-acre guarded prison. The executioner was its priest, the prison personnel worshippers, the district magistrate the chorister, and the cheerleaders were psychologists and sociologists of human behaviour.

The black mask covering his head and face added to the darkness of the entire world, and Thoma Kunj could imagine the noose hanging from the crossbar, sturdy, oval, and able to withstand the weight of the condemned. Two loops from the same horizontal beam for two convicted prisoners considerably reduced the prison authorities' workload. It took months, at times, years of preparation to hang a felon, as appeals to the high court, supreme court, and the president consumed many years and postponed capital punishment. Even after the rejection of the final appeal, months of preparation followed, and getting an executioner was onerous.

The gallows were the mightiest instrument humans invented to suppress the human spirit. It had the power to take away life, a tool to hang a person till death from the trap attached to a crossbar. That more than one snare operated simultaneously was a blessing for the judiciary, the government, and the prison personnel. The government used enormous funds to hang a convict, at least ten times more than the total requirement, to keep the offender in prison for a lifetime.

In prison, a felon could work, earn a livelihood, support his family, and strive for the country's development.

But suicide was different; it was a person's choice, and Emily chose her death.

Emily died on the cross.

Dying on a cross had religious glory and spiritual promise. But the victim had to be hanged, like Jesus of Nazareth. Emily hanged herself and lost her glory and promise. The vicar refused to bury her in the cemetery, and George Mooken bribed the vicar for a slice of mud. The priest allotted it in the Themmadi Kuzhi, the sinner's corner and Emily was buried with a black cloth as she had no right to be covered with a white sheet. Those covered with white sheets would go directly to heaven, and those with black to purgatory to be cleansed or to hell in eternal fire. The God of the Jews and Christians, Yahweh, loved white, and Allah's houris wore white Abayas. Both disliked black, the colour of Lucifer or

Iblis. The sons of Abraham treasured white, the colour of the angels, malaks and houris.

Emily's body, covered with a black sheet, was buried in the cemetery in the sinner's corner.

Not a sinner at birth, Emily was the only child of a teaching couple from Thiruvalla who taught English and Mathematics in Addis Ababa. Elizabeth and Jacob disliked having a child, but when thirty-eight, Elizabeth became pregnant and reached Rachel's house in Thiruvalla for the delivery. Within a day of the child's birth, Elizabeth returned to Ethiopia to be with her husband, not even asking her mother to raise the newborn. Rachel knew Elizabeth had abandoned her baby and would not return to see the child.

Her grandma brought Emily up and taught her to speak the Queen's English from day one. When Emily was four years old, Rachel taught her to write the alphabet in Malayalam and English. Emily called her "Mama."

For some years, Rachel was a surgeon in Birmingham, suffered from mild psychotic paranoia, and had daily conflicts with her husband, David, whom she met while they studied at Vellore Medical College. A psychiatrist in the UK, Dr David, divorced Rachel after ten years of marriage and married a white woman, Margaret, a failed model and actor. She had regularly visited David for psychiatric treatment.

With her only daughter Elizabeth, Rachel shifted to London and continued her practice, carrying vile hatred toward her ex-husband and his new wife in her secret self.

She feared darkness and thought her divorced husband and wife would strangulate her during lightless nights. Rachel never switched off the light during the night. Hallucinations overpowered her mind, and she wrestled with David, Margaret, and other imagined enemies.

In London, Rachel made much wealth from her practice and shifted to Thiruvalla when she was sixty-five. Within a year, Elizabeth came, and Emily was born.

Emily was a lonely toddler and grew up as a solitary child.

She grew up listening to her grandma's shouting and howling, especially after sunset. Mama quarrelled with her divorced husband, Dr David and his English wife, Margaret, every night, thinking she was still in Birmingham, as she often saw him hugging his client in his clinic.

Sometimes, Rachel showed aggression towards strangers during travel, especially in hotels and resorts. She disliked actors and models and thought they all were in love with David. Impulsive in her reactions, she remained aloof for days together, forgetting Emily was with her. Grandma sometimes expressed antisocial behaviour, and Emily felt extreme fear. Rachel hated women of high-class society who wore fashionable clothes and jewellery. But Rachel bought expensive dresses and diamonds for Emily without consulting her. Every day, Rachel pugnaciously attacked the giant rubberised dolls of Dr David and his wife she kept in her bedroom. After kicking in their face, she sat on their chest like a wrestler and punched them repeatedly.

"David, I hate you," she screeched.

"I hate you, David. You married that bitch. I will never forgive you," the shrieking would get louder.

"It is you who need psychiatric treatment, you bloody fool," the expletives continued.

Emily had a bedroom of her own, and during the uproar and yelling, Emily hid under her pillows, trembling with fear. With curiosity, Emily watched her grandmother check the locked doors half a dozen times, especially at night. She got up at midnight and verified whether the central door lock was intact. Intense irrational persistent feelings of fear and anger emerged within her every few hours, making her argumentative and defensive toward fictional criticism. Often Emily remained in her room, not appearing before her Mama.

Rachel never forgave her ex-husband and his actress wife.

During the day, Rachel was talkative and asked Emily to read aloud a passage from a storybook. Grandma encouraged Emily to read clearly and corrected her pronunciation.

Rachel dressed up as a woman from an elite family, meticulously following the latest fashion trends in London, cooked western food, acted like a British aristocrat and spoke the Queen's English. She drove her car, went with Emily to Kochi, Alappuzha, Kottayam, Munnar, Trivandrum, and Kanyakumari, and stayed in the best hotels.

When she was five years old, Emily was sent to a girls' boarding school in Kodaikanal, where she did not like the atmosphere. She had no friends, as she was afraid to talk to other students. Emily did not know who to accept as she grew up alone without siblings and parents. Emily grew up with an older woman who suffered from paranoia, schizoid and mental imbalances. Even though her teachers behaved with love and care, Emily kept a distance from them. Her grandmother visited the school every month, on the eve of Christmas and the midsummer holidays. Her sophisticated behaviour was always a talk among the schoolteachers, and Rachel's visits continued till Emily completed her matriculation.

Emily was good at her studies. Even though she was lonely, she was a compelling speaker and participated in inter and intra-school competitions. Every year, Emily went on a study tour with her classmates and visited significant tourist spots in India, Nepal, Bhutan and Sri Lanka, but without mingling with anyone.

She met her parents when she was nine years old, for the first time while with her grandma at Thiruvalla during the Christmas holidays. One afternoon, Emily saw two strangers, a man and a woman, getting out of a taxi in front of their house. Emily was astonished because they behaved like a newly married couple. Rachel was relatively indifferent to them. They did not talk to Emily or show any interest in her as if she had never existed, and Emily did not know who they were.

"Emily, meet your parents, the bastards from Ethiopia," Rachel shouted from the sitting room.

There was a long silence.

"You want to grab my property, but you get it only over my dead body," grandma bellowed from the sitting room.

Elizabeth and Jacob left within a half-hour.

"Go to hell, never return. I am already seventy-five. Let me have some peace," Rachel roared while they were going out.

Mama continued to shout throughout the evening; she was agitated. She kicked the dolls of David and Margaret. The shrieking and expletives filled the air, drowning out the carols.

Emily was a lonely child. She had no friends in the neighbourhood.

In her adolescence, her loneliness intensified. Suddenly there were hordes of pimples on my face. When she was twelve years old, menstruation started. Emily did not know it and had no one to speak to. Repeated distressing feelings accompanying the perception that something terrible had happened within her body crushed her emotions and comfort. Her nightdress was wet with blood, and she could not accept it as she did not know why it happened, what would happen to her, and where to throw away the nighty. She hid from other students in the dining hall and classroom and was afraid of standing in the general assembly or classroom. Her period continued for six days and eased her emotionally; a shame permeated her head with pain in her lower belly. Nausea, cramps, and bloated feelings agitated her, especially her breasts. There was a burning sensation in the nipples, and she pressed them repeatedly. Emily felt tired, weak and sluggish.

Mood changes made Emily angry and lost; anxiety oppressed her continuously as if she was travelling through a tunnel, there was no end to it, or there was no opening on the other side. She perceived standing on the peak of a mountain, and there was no way to climb down; the cliffs were too steep and dangerous. Emily was angry, and in her mind, she shouted at her teachers, her parents, her grandma and the whole world.

The next menstrual cycle was after four months. Emily was at home with her grandma, who was non-approachable, as she was cursing David and Margaret for days together. Emily never had an opportunity to speak to Mama about the biological and emotional changes. On the third day, after breakfast, Rachel saw drops of blood on the dining hall floor, and for the first time in Emily's life, grandma hugged her with concern and told her she had become a woman. Grandma explained to Emily, in the most straightforward words, all about the mystery of menstruation, the monthly period, the need to keep the body clean, how to use a pad, and the emotional and psychological preparations necessary to handle it.

For the next few weeks, every day, Grandma explained to Emily about the ovum being developed in her ovary, the rejection of the unfertilised ovum, sperms formed in male testicles, sexual intercourse between a female and a male, its biological and psychological undercurrents, the human fulfilment of sexual relationship, and how to avoid unwanted pregnancies. Rachel opined sex between a girl and boy was not a sin; in no way did it diminish the dignity of human life but enhanced it. Sexual rapport had specific social-psychological implications and personal and societal ramifications. Even though there was nothing wrong with premarital sex, grandma explicitly told Emily how to circumvent unwanted pregnancies, discouraging a boy from having predatory sex. For Mama, sex was a natural biological phenomenon interrelated to a person's emotional and psychological needs and growth. Emily needed to be prudent in developing sexual unions with a male.

"Religion and God have nothing to do with sex. Religion is a social construct, and God is a myth; they can't interfere in human affairs. Throw away both of them. Sex is purely biological with psychological, emotional and social consequences, and you should be responsible for your body, mind, and future. Be judicious in dealing with males," grandma said, looking at Emily.

"Mama, I will follow what you said," Emily replied.

"I won't force you, Emily; you are responsible for your actions," Rachel said.

I understand, Mama."

"If there is no God, humans are responsible for their actions," Rachel said.

Grandma was talking about sex and God for the first time. Emily felt thankful to her for making her understand the meaning of biological womanhood and freedom from God.

Emily joined for her two-year senior secondary in a school in Trivandrum after completing her tenth class; she was fifteen. The school was for both boys and girls and the first opportunity for Emily to mingle with boys, but she was reluctant to develop a friendship with them. She never had a chance to talk to a boy. In grandma's house, Emily felt alone, never meeting a boy in the neighbourhood. Her boarding school was for girls, and all teachers and administrative staff were women. Even though she was curious about boys, she never had an experience mingling with them. Emily dreamt of watching the naked body of a boy; she wanted to see a penis, touch it, feel it, to know how it behaved, as she had not once seen one. Emily thought about it for many weeks and had delusions of playing with the genitals of a boyfriend.

She developed repeated distressing feelings and the perception that her social and emotional needs were not met as a child as she desired. She was sad about being lonely, being away from boys. Not having boys with her to touch and caress saddened her as boys in the class were strangers to her, but they looked handsome and vigorous. But phantasms of being followed by a boy scared her, and she was always stressed about her sexual urges and spent sleepless nights thinking about having male companions. Depression and anxiety oppressed her.

In school, she could not connect with other students and teachers, as she lacked a best friend with whom she could share her deepest thoughts, which helped her remove self-doubt and lack of self-worth.

At home, during the holidays, most of her time was spent ruminating on the company of a boyfriend. As Mama was above eighty, she could not bother about the changes taking place in Emily. Constantly feeling empty, there was a hidden longing for someone to hug her, have sex with her, and take care of her. She chose to be secluded but unhappy about her aloneness, wished she had a loving male who cared for her like a friend, with whom she could travel all over the world, talk about anything under the sun, and have lasting intimate moments.

Sexual urge drummed her head like rain on a tin-top shack; she shut her room and remained inside, feeling inadequate, saddened to be inside and alone. She had nothing to talk to her grandma at the table; she felt miserable sharing with the older woman who shook her hand while holding the fork and knife. Different emotions oppressed Emily as she loved her grannie and hated her for looking after her as a baby, as it was better to strangulate her as soon as she was born.

Emily felt scared while watching grandma thrashing the dolls. David and Margaret might have experienced pain when the old woman repeatedly punched them.

For Emily, her secondary school was empty, albeit alive with students. During elocution competitions, she thought no one would listen to her even though the hall was overflowing with an audience who admired her ability to speak cogently, logically and convincingly. She started talking to remove her loneliness and won prizes to chase away her solitude.

In isolation, Emily felt sexually starved; at times, the urge was uncontrollable, which forced her to think and thinking led to more loneliness, centred on a friend who could relieve her sexual need. But her feelings were not linked to the reality of the situation because they were often fleeting like stray clouds, purposeless and goalless, but tied to her life in such a way she tried to escape from it.

Often, she felt jealous of other students because they enjoyed the company of their friends. In contrast, Emily had no one to share her emotions and desires with, as she was insufficiently allied with others. She thought her situation would never end as she would be unwanted, unloved, insecure and abandoned. A lingering sadness emerged that she failed to define, but it was because of a lack of a person to love her, and she wanted to return that love. It would be a caring, built-in profound understanding of the need of some intimate.

Emily wanted to belong but was afraid of belonging.

Her emotions were focused on achieving her deep-felt need. She searched for a man to be with her, breathe within her, feel with her, and create endless passionate joy.

Excluded from her parents, Emily searched for a person like a father, a lover, and a boyfriend. Her parents were total strangers with whom she never talked, and she did not even know what parenthood was. That created an unbridgeable gap in her life, and only a man could bridge it. The concept of father shaped an emptiness in her, an unending wilderness, a vast ocean of darkness, an emptiness of love in its totality.

A father did not exist for her.

Emily was excluded from her father's care, and often she felt highly motivated to find a person who could accept her.

Silence possessed her, and fear enveloped her, filling her heart and mind with emptiness and darkness without a boundary. Sometimes she became obscurity personified; there was nothing to think and expect, a strong desire for someone, a male. Everything ended in a void without hope; there was nowhere to go, no vehicle to travel, and no road to lead. It was like a mirage in the desert, and Emily was unaccompanied. She disliked crying and detested feeling sad, as her life was empty as a coconut shell.

When she completed her senior secondary school, Emily joined a women's college in Ernakulam for graduation; she was eighteen and selected English, her favourite subject, for the degree, a three-year course. Rachel was eighty-four and opened a savings bank account for Emily with an initial deposit of twenty lakh rupees to complete her studies without financial burden.

Emily started staying in the hostel and visited her Mama once a month, much mellowed down with age but still queenly, moody and silent.

In the college, Emily was a member of the Public Speaking Forum and was responsible for inviting guests to preside over various functions organised by the Forum. In one of the functions, she requested a young lawyer, Mohan, a dynamic speaker who could fuse law and literature succinctly. Soon, Emily started to like and admire Mohan, visited his office and engaged in lengthy discussions. Rapidly, Emily was lifted to a new world of male proximity, warmth and smell, and she revered it, fulfilling her dreams since her adolescence. Emily adored Mohan, his looks, constant word flow, general knowledge, concern, and respect for Emily. Many evenings, she sat close to him and looked into his eyes as if possessed by his male vigour, power and magic.

During weekends, Emily and Mohan visited the best restaurants in Kochi and spent long hours in each other's company. Cash flowed from her purse, and she was contented to pay Mohan to keep him pleased and excited. Every evening, he selected a bottle of expensive whiskey and felt glad that Emily paid for it joyfully. For the first time, Emily closely interacted with a man, and she liked everything in Mohan's behaviour, including his looks and smell. She desired to hug him, keeping him close to her heart. It was a novelty for Emily to be with a man, cuddling him in her arms. The power of new ideas of togetherness erupted within her.

They regularly took a boat for a joy ride and travelled up to Alappuzha, Changanassery, and Kumarakom. Spending time with Mohan was a heavenly experience for Emily.

The ecstasy of emotions made her speechless; her passion exploded as she could feel dreams dancing in her belly.

Emily felt adventurous, doing anything to please Mohan, curious about his reactions and appearance. With new ideas about living together, she told him countless stories, forgot about her other priorities, craved sex and mentally enjoyed being with Mohan naked. A basket of physical and psychological responses in her actions and interactions forced her into an addictive dependence on him and a stronger desire for lovemaking. She loved to be crushed by him when she was with him.

A vital concern for Mohan emerged in her heart, filling every moment of her existence with a desire to make his life easier with the latest gadgets, gifting him costly items that might make him smile. Prioritising her decisions based on his likes and dislikes, she carried him within her constantly like a newly pregnant woman protecting her zygote.

She recollected repeatedly meeting him for the first time in his office, an overwhelming experience, standing close to him and the germination of a solid physical and emotional attraction and attachment. Even on the first day, she wanted to see him in the nude, briefly doubting whether she had lost her clarity, the consilience.

Day after day, Emily was evolving, an entirely new person, feeling emotional with physical changes; there were high palpitations and obsessive thinking at times. Her reactions were instant but encircled in nervousness, a penetrating feeling of joy coupled with distrust as she experienced it so strongly. The sentiments and responses were solid and advanced quickly, leading to a loss of judgment and crazy decisions lacking logical results.

Mohan stayed alone in a house overlooking the Vembanad lake, and one evening he took Emily to his house. It was a one-bedroom flat with a small sitting room and a tiny kitchen, and she loved it as she found it cosy and compact, where Emily was alone with a man she admired and loved. She had sex for the first time as soon as they reached; she loved the naked body of Mohan, the way he hugged, undressed, and kissed her. The freshness of everything riveted her, and the slight pain caused by the sexual union was a lovely experience; her obsession with sex intensified. On the next day, Emily shifted to Mohan's place from her hostel.

Emily loved Mohan. His charm enchanted her, and she liked how he was doing everything. Making love challenged her concept of a man-woman relationship, and Emily thought about how lucky she was to have a friend like Mohan, who prized and cared for her so much. She wondered how to thank Mohan for the heavenly bliss he gave her.

The next day, Emily took Mohan to a car showroom and presented a car where she felt so close to him. Mohan hugged her with joy and kissed her lips. They regularly travelled to Mysore, Bangalore, Goa, Ooty, Kodaikanal and Chennai, and Emily was glad to spend any amount for her beloved boyfriend.

She was thrilled to hear from Mama she had deposited another ten lakh rupees in her account as a gift, and Emily shared the exciting news with Mohan and told him he was free to operate her bank for his needs.

Mohan took an extended leave for two months, telling Emily he loved to be with her in the initial days of intimacy. He would start the law practice after the euphoria of their inseparability subsided. Emily hugged him and kissed him for his concern.

Mohan planned a foreign tour for Emily and him to Java, Bali, Kuala Lumpur, Bangkok, Angkor Wat and Saigon. The visit was for four weeks.

Without informing Mama from Kochi, Emily and Mohan took a direct flight to Kuala Lumpur, where they spent four days visiting almost all prominent tourist attractions. Emily loved the inventiveness of everything. In Bali, they had lovely days, and Emily played with Mohan on the beach like a little child. Bangkok mesmerised her, especially its nightlife. Thousands of white people walking in minimum clothing engrossed Emily, and she told Mohan they must be like those tourists when they return home within their privacy. The grandeur of Angkor Wat charmed her, and Saigon enchanted her.

Emily loved Mohan's possessive nature; he was like a young father.

When they returned to India, they went directly to Mohan's house. While checking her bank accounts, Emily became jubilant as Rachel had deposited another five lakhs. Even though she had already spent about eighteen lakhs, her bank had a balance of seventeen lakhs.

On a Saturday, she took a bus from Kochi to Thiruvalla to meet Mama. When reaching home, Emily found another family staying in the house. They said her grandma died two weeks ago, and Elizabeth and Jacob sold the house to the present occupants. The new owners did not allow Emily to enter the house; she stood outside and wept, remembering Mama.

Emily had no place to go except the house of Mohan, and on return, she narrated the whole story. Mohan did not say a word. There was silence in the house for many days. Without telling Emily, he went to court by car and resumed practice. Emily started attending college, and when she returned, she was alone at home and had no one to talk to. Within fifteen days, she felt uneasy and asked Mohan to accompany her to a doctor. But Mohan expressed his inability as he had a critical case that day and would not go with her.

Emily went alone.

After a detailed diagnostic examination, the lady's physician told Emily she was pregnant. Emily experienced ecstasy; now, everything had changed, a new meaning, colours, and responsibilities. She waited for Mohan to return, and as soon as he arrived around six in the evening, Emily informed him with a smile she was pregnant. She expected Mohan would hug her and kiss her with joy. But he did not react, said nothing; a profound silence pervaded all corners of the house, dismantling her trust in Mohan.

The following morning, Mohan went to his office without informing Emily, and Emily felt strange; she took a bus to her college. When Emily tried to transfer an amount to pay her semester fees, she found only fifty thousand rupees in her account. In the evening, when she told Mohan an amount of sixteen and a half lakh rupees had disappeared from her bank, he said he had taken the money for some urgent need and was there to look after Emily in all her needs.

Emily trusted Mohan and believed in his words.

That morning after Emily left for college, Mohan locked the house with a new padlock and went to his office. When Emily came back from college at six in the evening, Mohan had not returned from the court. As the keys to the main door were with Mohan, she waited. It became dark, and Emily waited outside beyond ten. Mohan's car reached home around half-past ten. He opened the door and went inside, and Emily followed him. Mohan asked Emily to sleep in the sitting room, feeling strange. In the sitting room, she could not sleep comfortably.

The following day, Mohan told Emily she needed to abort the baby, and he had made all arrangements in an abortion clinic. Emily could not believe his words.

"You are only eighteen, too young to be a mother," he said.

"But I want to keep the baby," she replied.

"We cannot afford a child now," Mohan said.

"You have a good practice and are earning sufficiently well," Emily argued.

"I need the money to buy a house," he said.

Emily looked at Mohan with wary eyes.

"You had told me this house belonged to you," Emily replied.

"Don't question me," Mohan screamed, and the threat implicit in his words reverberated in her ears and coalesced with her loneliness and silence.

It was a warning; Emily became frightened and grappled with fear; Mohan was a changed man, or he had started showing his real nature.

Emily kept quiet. But she was upset and wanted to save the child at any cost. She tried to escape from Mohan; nonetheless, she had no options. Her bank balance was almost nil, and there was no possibility of earning a livelihood; there was no place to go and no relatives. She felt hapless; suddenly, the world changed, and she felt terrified.

The following day, Mohan told her they would be shifting to a new house within two days, and she needed an abortion before that. Emily was silent.

"Speak," Mohan raised his voice.

"I don't want to abort my baby," she murmured.

"Obey what I say," he shouted while slapping her twice.

Those were heavy blows; blood oozed out from her nose. There was darkness for a few seconds; she felt like she was falling to the ground. The pain was unbearable; it was for the first time someone had hit her. While washing her face under the tap, Emily tasted blood. She covered her nose with a handkerchief, which became thoroughly wet with blood within a few minutes. Emily cried aloud, but Mohan feigned deafness.

She went to the sitting room and tried to lie down; the excruciating pain and bleeding made her uneasy, and while grappling with the truth, she lost consciousness for a few minutes.

That day Emily did not go to college, but Mohan left for court.

In the afternoon, a well-built woman came to see Emily. She drove Mohan's car and told Emily Mohan had asked her to take Emily to their new house, where he would be waiting for them. Emily had a lingering doubt but went with her. On the way, both of them did not talk. The woman was driving through a crowded area, a marketplace, and after half an hour, there was a traffic jam. The car stopped for another half an hour. The woman was impatient and got out of the car, saying there was an accident, and walked ahead to find out whether she could drive on.

Emily looked through the window. On both sides, there were hundreds of shops and other establishments. It was not a residential area, and she was sure the woman was taking her elsewhere. She could see a large board with red background about two hundred metres ahead, written: "ABORTION CLINIC". Emily got a shiver through her spine; it spread throughout her body, shattering her illusion. Without thinking much, she opened the door and disappeared among the crowd.

Except for her handbag, Emily had nothing with her. She walked fast and took a pocket road, a part of the old Kochi. She ran for an hour and was already on the seashore. Hundreds of fisherwomen were there selling fish, squatting on the ground on both sides of the road.

Beyond that were the large Chinese nets; the sun was burning, humid air, and the sea was strangely calm. The smell of fried fish in coconut oil filled the air. She walked fast, covering her head with her dupatta, but she did not know where to go or what to do.

She had never been to that area.

Emily was alone in the teaming crowd, lonely like a stray cat, fearful and timid, and had nobody in the world and no place to call her own. Blood continued dripping from her nose; her fingers were slightly wet with blood when she wiped the nose. Darkness was evolving in her eyes; her head was heavy; she sat by the side of the road where a middle-aged woman was selling fish. She sat there for a long time as if she could not move, feeling dizzy and unwell. There were some customers; the woman was busy weighing, cleaning, cutting and packing, totally engaged in her work. Her daughter arranged fish according to their variety, size and colour. More and more customers came, bought fish, and went away, some alone, some in small groups, couples; there was always bargaining. It was interesting to watch them as all were busy, and everyone had a place to go back, someone waiting for someone. Slowly, the number of customers diminished, one or two came in long intervals, and then there were none. Emily sat there and watched the mother and daughter, a happy duo, fully engaged in their work. They had sold almost everything, and their shop was nearly empty, with only a few pieces of small fish left.

"Mama, let's go; there are no more customers," the girl, about twelve years, said while collecting the leftovers in a small basket.

'What's the time?" the woman asked the girl.

"It's half past ten," the girl replied.

The street was practically vacant by now; a few fisherwomen left; they, too, were collecting the scraps in their baskets and folding the plastic sheets on which they displayed the fish they sold.

"Why are you sitting here? Haven't you bought any fish?" the woman asked Emily.

"No, I haven't bought any," said Emily.

"Then why are you here?" asked the woman.

Emily looked at the woman; she was about forty, heavily built, and wearing a loose dress to her knees. Her eyes were big and dark, had a prominent nose and large lips. While talking, her teeth were shown clearly.

"I have nowhere to go," said Emily.

The woman looked at Emily for a few seconds to evaluate Emily's words and looks.

"What happened to you? I can see blood oozing from your nose," the woman inquired.

"I had a fall," Emily replied.

By now, the girl had finished her work; The baskets were intact, the plastic sheets folded, and the knives were carefully packed in a leather pouch and tied safely.

"If you have no place, where will you sleep," the girl asked, looking at Emily. There was concern in her voice.

"Don't remain here during the night; it is not safe," the woman said.

Emily did not say anything.

"Mama, let her come with us. She can sleep in our house," said the girl.

The woman looked at Emily once again.

"Come with us," the woman said.

She helped Emily to get up. Even though her hands were cold, her touch was warm and firm. The girl started walking, carrying the baskets where she kept the leather bag. She held two buckets in her right hand; within them, the unsold fish. The woman took the folded plastic sheet on her head.

"Give me the buckets; I can hold them," Emily said to the girl.

The girl looked at Emily.

"Every day, I do it. After school, I come here around six in the evening and sit with mama till ten-thirty," said the girl.

"But today, I can hold it," said Emily.

The girl gave the buckets with fish to Emily, and Emily felt good, as if she had become a part of the family. They walked through the seashore for about fifteen minutes and reached a cluster of long sheds, six of them; each shelter had ten houses, and the mother and daughter stayed in the fifth shack, the second house. The house was painted white, kept clean and had a sitting room, a bedroom, a kitchen, and a toilet in a corner.

The woman's husband was bedridden; he was a truck driver, and once during the monsoon, while climbing the Western Ghats, his truck fell into a ravine. His spinal cord was broken, and he was incapacitated for eight years. The daughter looked after her father like a nurse. The woman was considerate and loving towards her husband.

The woman showed Emily the bathroom. Emily washed her clothes, took a warm water bath, and wore a nighty given by the girl. Around midnight, they had dinner together, with warm rice, fried fish, and vegetables. Emily slept on the sitting room floor on a mattress covered with a cotton sheet. The night was cold, and she covered herself with a thin blanket. Emily slept well. When she got up around six in the morning, the woman was busy in the kitchen, and the girl was studying. By seven, they had their breakfast—puttu, kadala curry, banana and filter coffee. The woman told Emily that by eight in the morning, she would be going to the seashore to buy fish and go to the door-to-door selling and would be back by one in the afternoon, cook food, feed her husband and again by three would purchase fish and go to the fish-street and sell it till ten-thirty night. The girl would go to school around nine and return by four in the evening. She would be helping her mother from six.

The woman had prepared two food packets in a paper lunchbox covered with white paper.

"Please take it; you may feel hungry; on your way, wherever you go, you can eat it," she said.

"Thank you so much. I don't know what to say," Emily said.

"I have kept fifty rupees within the bag; that would be enough for your expenses for two days, besides your bus charges," the woman said while giving her a small shoulder bag with some fresh clothes and two bottles of water.

Emily wept. Her heart was filled with gratitude.

"Bye," the girl said.

"Have a good time," the woman wished.

Emily walked and thought of going to Alappuzha, fifty-three kilometres away. She did not want to take a bus within the city, so she took a small truck going south. Within an hour, she got another truck going to Kuttanad vis Alappuzha to bring back live ducks to the city. The seat next to the driver was vacant, and he offered it to Emily without charging a fee. Within an hour, they reached Alappuzha, and Emily thought of going to the duck farms about ten to fifteen kilometres.

In Kuttanad, there were hundreds of duck farmers. Emily went to see six duck yards with the driver, where the driver purchased four hundred ducks. The farmer had more than fifteen hundred ducks, besides about five hundred ducklings. Emily asked him whether he could give her a job.

The farmer, his wife and their two children were active in duck farming, and two full-time workers took ducks to various paddy fields during the day. Once the eggs were hatched and the ducklings were out, they constantly moved from one paddy field to another for twelve months. Many ducks laid eggs in the fields, and the workers collected them in baskets. In the evening, they brought back the eggs to the yard with the ducks. Some ducks laid eggs in the yard. Ducks older than twelve months were sold for meat.

After consulting his wife, the farmer offered a job to Emily for a monthly remuneration of five hundred rupees with accommodation in a hut attached to the duck yard, which had a room, a platform for cooking and a tiny toilet. Emily was happy to get the job offer, and her work consisted of packing eggs in eggboxes and sealing them within the name of that specific farm. Every day there were about seven hundred-fifty to eight hundred eggs. Emily had to maintain the account book on eggs and the live birds sold to different agencies, the money received, the salary paid, the feed purchased and other expenses.

The paddy farmers of Kuttanad encouraged duck farming as it was lucrative. Ducks did not need a roosting space, but they were kept in an enclosed area known as a duck yard, adjacent to the paddy field and close to the house, protected from predators. Emily liked the work, and she remained busy the whole day. The farmer's wife was friendly; she gave Emily cooked food, including duck curry, fried fish, and different rice preparations, almost every day. Once she knew Emily was pregnant, she regularly took her to a gynaecologist for consultation and medical assistance.

Suddenly, bird flu spread over Kuttanad when Emily completed seven months in the farmer's family.

It spread fast, and thousands of ducks died every day. The government sent volunteers to cull the birds in the affected area. On Emily's farm, practically all ducks were culled within three days, and their carcasses burned in the field. Soon, Emily became jobless, and the farmer lost lakhs of rupees. The farmer's wife told Emily she could stay with her, and they would meet all expenses for her delivery. But Emily did not want to burden them and left them early the next day.

She took a boat to Kumarakom in search of work, as there were many houseboats and restaurants; hundreds of tourists from abroad and from different states of India visited the tourist spots around the backwaters of Kuttanad. As she was pregnant, many houseboats and restaurants rejected her plea for a job. Emily wandered on the road looking for a job till evening. When it was dark, she spotted a wayside restaurant thatched with palm leaves, run by a woman and her husband. They were both Bengali. They had two toddlers. Emily asked them whether she could work with them to serve tea and food to customers, including washing and cleaning utensils. The couple was kind and told her they were ready to provide her with a job, and she could eat and sleep there.

The restaurant was mainly for Bengali food; most customers were labourers from Bengal, Odisha and Assam, who came for breakfast, lunch and dinner. Rice, various fish preparations, different types of sweets and tea were the main items on the menu. Emily's job was serving food cooked by the woman. Her husband cleaned the restaurant, washed the utensils and did the purchasing. Emily ate with the couple and slept on the floor. Emily's days with them were happy as her employers treated her with respect and concern.

Then the police squad came; they were ruthless. As the restaurant was constructed on the roadside, on Porompokku, government land, the police dismantled the shed within ten minutes and burned it. Nothing was left; even the utensils were destroyed. The Bengali couple lost everything; their children stood on the road and wept.

The woman hugged Emily, wept, and gave her five hundred rupees for the work for two months.

Emily walked to Kottayam, a distance of about fifteen kilometres. She had nine hundred and fifty rupees in her purse and thought of admitting herself to a maternity hospital there. After about five kilometres, a car stopped in front of her; a woman in the car asked Emily where she was going, and she replied she was going to Jubilee Park, Kottayam, as she knew there were a couple of maternity hospitals nearby. The woman helped her enter the car and was at Jubilee Park within fifteen minutes. When she came out of the car, Emily felt tired; she wanted to sit again. She strolled into the park and sat on a bench for hours. When Kurien, a dark, short man, stood before her, she knew someone was there to help her. Kurien had a heart full of empathy. When the Karnataka police assaulted Kurien and killed him, they could not see a vibrant hub that loved Emily and Thoma Kunj; for them, love for a family was immaterial and non-existent. With each blow on his face, chest and belly, they constructed the gallows for Emily, and her scaffold was a cross that stood in front of her church in Ayyankunnu. Thoma Kunj saw her hanging over the naked Jesus, who died two thousand years ago on the outskirts of Jerusalem. Kurien died on the Mysore Kannur highway near Makkoottam within the forest, and Emily was before the believers of Christ.

Thoma Kunj's gallows were constructed in independent India, where voiceless murder convicts were hanged, but the vocal ones became politicians and ministers. The gallows stood there in the name of Hammurabi, Bentham and Mohan. The gallows had two nooses for two convicts; Thoma Kunj knew it when he had overheard lifers talking about it. The government used the gallows against its citizens, like the guillotine in George Mooken's abattoir for the pigs. But on the gallows, humans were the pigs.

Chapter Six

THE NOOSE

Odysseus and his son Telemachus hanged twelve maids on the gallows by loops, as they thought their servants were disloyal to Odysseus in his absence. The teacher explained a passage from the Odyssey in the ninth class, and Thoma Kunj was attentive.

"Who is the author of Odyssey, and in which language did he write?" the teacher asked Ambika.

"The author of Odyssey is Homer, and he wrote in Greek," Ambika answered.

What type of literature is Odyssey?" The question was directed to Appu.

Appu looked around, as he had no answer. The teacher repeated the question and asked Thoma Kunj to answer it.

"It is an epic poem," said Thoma Kunj.

Who can say what was the central theme of Odyssey?" Looking at everyone, the teacher questioned.

"There was silence in the class as if the students were in deep reflection; Thoma Kunj raised his right hand, and the teacher permitted him to speak.

"There are three main themes in Odyssey—hospitality, loyalty and vengeance," explained Thoma Kunj.

"You have answered well; where did you learn it?" the teacher queried while congratulating him.

"My mother had told me the stories of many epics, the Mahabharata, Ramayana, Odyssey, Silappathikaram, Epic of Gilgamesh, and Paradise Lost. She was a good storyteller, and I learned many lessons from her," Thoma Kunj narrated.

The teacher and other students listened to him in silence. They knew Emily had died a year ago, and Thoma Kunj continued his studies despite being depressed. On weekends and holidays, he worked in the pigsty of George Mooken, though George Mooken and Parvathy expressed their readiness to adopt him. But Thoma Kunj insisted on living independently and working to earn his livelihood.

Emily recounted the story of Odysseus, the King of Ithaca. The epics reiterated his struggles to return home after the Trojan war and his heroics when he reunited with his wife Penelope and son Telemachus. Homer was influenced by the concepts of fate, gods, and free will. Humans were endowed with free will and responsible for their actions, which was the central philosophy of the epic. The notion of free will was the central pillar of Greek thoughts that influenced western ideas on human freedom. Religions, philosophies, literature, law, and politics developed and flourished based on free will. Besides that, some distinct forces shaped the lives of humans, such as piety, customs, justice, memory, grief, glory, and honour, but they were subservient to free will. It was lovely to listen to Emily recounting the stories, and Thoma Kunj sat by her side and was engrossed in her words.

"We are responsible for our actions to a great extent, but not completely," Emily said.

"Why are we not responsible?" Thoma Kunj raised a query.

"We are products of nature and nurture. Certain things within and around us form us; we cannot change them, only accept them. In some aspects of our lives, we are the creators, so we can change and be responsible for those actions," Emily elaborated.

Thoma Kunj had a different opinion.

Free will was a contradiction. If humans were free, they would be determined to be free, and they could not be free. If humans were not free, they were bound to be not free, and free will could not exist. Humans were like the livestock in the pigsty of George Mooken; they never asked to be born, were never interested in being castrated, and never wished to be guillotined. The world was an enormous abattoir God created, and each human was a piglet to be castrated to enter heaven. God created heaven and earth, a mystery for Thoma Kunj; either heaven or earth was sufficient, and both were unnecessary. God should have restrained himself from testing humans on earth before pushing them into heaven or hell. Thoma Kunj laughed silently when he thought about it, alone at home.

"Do you believe in heaven and hell?" Thoma Kunj asked Ambika, his best friend, while they were walking to school.

No," said Ambika.

"Why?" Thoma Kunj questioned.

"My father told me all religions are based on fake stories, not historical facts. Like Odyssey, each religion developed from the imagination of its writers and founders, as our teacher explained in class."

"Then what is not fake?" Thoma Kunj asked.

"For my father, communism alone is not false. It is the voice of the underprivileged, the oppressed, the workers." Ambika replied.

"Do you trust your father's words?" asked Thoma Kunj.

"Of course, he doesn't tell lies," Ambika said with conviction.

Thoma Kunj wanted to ask Ambika why his father and his friends raided the houses of their political opponents, cutting them into pieces with hatchets or throwing country-made bombs in their places. There were many killings all over Kerala by the youth wing in which Ambika's father was active, and others retaliated or sometimes initiated violence. But Thoma Kunj did not ask Ambika as he did not want to hurt her.

Ambika's father was Kannur's leading party worker, with hundreds of youths under him to do anything for him and his bosses. Many of his companions had no work as they were always busy with agitations, protests, burning public properties, violence and killings. Small-scale industries, educational institutions, and other political parties' youth wing were their targets. Due to their efforts, many industries shut their doors in Kerala, and Ambika's father and his followers celebrated their victory with alcohol and tandoori chicken. Unemployment and underemployment were necessary to enrol disenchanted youth into their fold. They spoke loudly against the US and secretly tried to get a green card at any cost. Their elite often visited UAE, European countries and the United States for business and expert medical treatment. Some indulged in the smuggling of drugs, gold and luxury items.

Thoma Kunj had seen scores of young men wandering house to house with buckets to collect cash and packed food. By evening, their buckets were full. There was no compulsion to give money, but those reluctant to pay experienced the young brigades' arm-twisting tactics.

Amika shared many stories about her father with Thoma Kunj while walking together to school. She trusted him and loved him. Ambika was in the class when Thoma Kunj hit Appu.

Thoma Kunj was responsible for his action, the school headmaster declared, as he hit Appu's face, and his teeth fell. That was the first and last time Thoma Kunj got wild with someone. He could not control himself; the reaction was beyond what he expected. No one inquired what provoked Thoma Kunj, a well-behaved youngster with no violent history. None cared about Appu's foul mouth.

"Your mother was a veshya," Appu said to Thoma Kunj in the class when the teacher was absent. He was jealous of Thoma Kunj, as he was a good student, answered almost all questions in the class, and spoke English rather well. What incited Appu was that Thoma Kunj could answer the queries raised by the teacher, saying that his mother had described stories of different epics. Appu was burning with jealousy; he was determined to humiliate Thoma Kunj before all students, especially the girls. Appu knew Thoma Kunj had a special affection for Ambika, and he waited for an opportunity to mortify Thoma Kunj before her. The best thing to do was speak ill of Thoma Kunj's dead mother. Appu had heard from his friend the vicar called her a veshya in his Sunday sermon. For Appu, that was the most befitting word to scorn Thoma Kunj.

Thoma Kunj was taller, more muscular and stouter than Appu. Kurien was short, and Appu had already raised questions about why Thoma Kunj's father did not look like him. He laughed loudly, which Thoma Kunj hated, but he had no ill will towards Appu.

"Thoma Kunj, don't be arrogant; everyone knows about your father and mother. Even Ambika knew that your mother was a veshya," Appu roared, and the whole class looked at Thoma Kunj. He disliked anyone speaking ill of his parents, especially about his mother. She was a good woman with a golden heart, loved him beyond words, and he could never accept anybody humiliating her. As courage personified, she fought against evil in society, those who cheated her and wounded her. Thoma Kunj's eyes were burning with rage. He balled his hands up into a fist; Thoma Kunj hit Appu's face with all his strength.

Appu fell unconscious and was immediately taken to the primary health care centre by the teachers. Within a day, his father filed a case at the police station against Thoma Kunj, the class teacher and headmaster. Appu was shifted to a hospital within a day and remained there for two weeks. There were surgeries to straighten his teeth, gum and lips.

The headmaster roared; his eyes bulged out. It was the first time that Thoma Kunj was in his cabin. A few other teachers were there; none expressed any sympathy towards Thoma Kunj, as if calling his mother a prostitute was not evil and had no consequences. Thoma Kunj did not look at the teachers as he could read their reactions. His class teacher was there, who often appreciated Thoma Kunj's performance in class and on tests. But the class teacher too was silent.

"Why did you hit Appu?" the headmaster thundered.

Appu abused his dead mother and called her a prostitute was the reply, and Thoma Kunj thought that it was a solid answer, sufficient to wipe out his guilt. Appu was from a better-off family; he had parents to oversee his welfare. But Thoma Kunj was an orphan; he had no one other than Parvathy and George Mooken. Those who had parents were stronger; Thoma Kunj knew it well. Even a tiger cub in the Ayyankunnu forest could not lead an orphaned life; hyenas waited to devour it. He had seen an elephant calf about six months old, without a mother, at the Dubare Elephant Camp near Kushalnagara. It was lonely and helpless, like a man not knowing swimming in the floodwaters of Barapuzha. Being bright or scoring high grades in-class tests was not sufficient; what was needed was the support and protection of parents. Thoma Kunj was lonely, like a pie dog or a hog taken to the guillotine.

"Don't try to defend yourself," the headmaster shouted.

Thoma Kunj looked at him. He had a cane in his right hand.

There was blow after blow on his back and buttocks. Someone was caning Thoma Kunj for the first time, and the cane recurrently fell on him as if skinning him. No teacher pleaded for mercy, and no one cared for his pain. Half a dozen grown-up males were blaring and bellowing.

Thoma Kunj felt hurt as no teacher reacted against the caning.

"Don't beat me," Thoma Kunj pleaded.

Suddenly there was silence. It was like the stillness after a thunder.

"What did you say? How dare you command the school's headmaster?" the class teacher shrieked.

The class teacher continued the caning on Thoma Kunj's shoulders and chest.

"Don't defend yourself. What you have done was a serious offence," the class teacher screamed while thrashing Thoma Kunj.

"Don't defend yourself, don't defend yourself, don't defend yourself," Thoma Kunj heard its echo a thousand times. The walls of the school building reverberated it cyclically.

"Stop it!" Parvathy cried, rushing inside the cabin. It was an order.

The teachers looked at her in disbelief, and there was total silence.

"How heartless are you? You cruel men, beating a child like a mad dog. He has done something wrong, but that does not mean you can form a criminal gang to thrash him. You have no right to skin him so cruelly. He is an orphan; it doesn't mean you have a licence to kill him." Parvathy's words were like wind hitting against the mighty Sahyadri with an unprecedented force, uprooting trees and shaking the rocks.

Parvathy led Thoma Kunj to her jeep and sped away.

Within a day, the magistrate of the juvenile justice court took custody of Thoma Kunj. Immediately, George Mooken and Parvathy reached the court and vouched for his good behaviour. The magistrate released Thoma Kunj under George Mooken and Parvathy's care and protection.

Thoma Kunj was bedridden for a month. Parvathy remained with him day and night, cooked his food, and fed and cared for him. She arranged for a doctor to visit him every day and a home nurse to take care of him.

Within a month, Thoma Kunj received communication from the school, rusticating him. Soon, George Mooken rushed to the school, but the headmaster was adamant. George Mooken pleaded with the headmaster to give Thoma Kunj a transfer certificate to join another school; nonetheless, the headmaster rejected his appeal.

That was the end of Thoma Kunj's education; his dream was to become an engineer, and he cried for many days. It wasn't easy to imagine a life without education, gaining knowledge and not acquiring a professional degree. Persistent distress enveloped him with a feeling of failure; it was like the mist covering the Ayyankunnu for days, surrounding the hills, spreading over the coconut and rubber trees. Thoma Kunj cried like a piglet subjected to castration as he could not believe the worst fate befell him. He had nightmares of fighting against massive creatures that wanted to scoff at him. Brooded over the responsibility of his actions, he spent sleepless nights feeling ashamed of himself. Humiliation overpowered him as if he had done something brazen, rather wicked, which had no payback. There was no escape, and he had to suffer throughout his life without any redemption as the burden of life was all-pervading, oppressive and gigantic.

Thoma Kunj felt crushed under an impasse without any hope and became frightened of his fate. He considered defending his actions, but the class teacher's words smashed him like a hailstorm, a precursor of a cyclone, which uprooted even coconut trees. At times, remorse over hitting Appu conquered him for many days, and Thoma Kunj repeatedly punched himself in the face. A sense of not being good enough crushed him, and he shouted: "I will never defend myself, whatever the cost." It was a vow, an oath taken in his mother's name, Emily.

Depression wrinkled his thoughts.

A man was not for defending himself but for others. But he would be lost in the quagmire of others' selfishness. Humans were selfish and tried to save themselves. It was a distressing feeling, and Thoma Kunj was conscious of his emotions, something constantly burning in his chest, a volcano that could erupt at any time. He wondered whether his decision not to defend himself was a prudent one, a rational choice. Was it a replication, an echo of his failures and distress? The constant anxiety about his decision broke him into a thousand pieces. He felt muscle tension all over his body and experienced difficulty walking, doing anything, even eating and lying down. Parvathy asked him to concentrate on his daily routine and leave his mind free from tragic events that happened in his life. Thoma Kunj looked at Parvathy for a long time, but he had no words to express his anxieties and worries, and his mind was illogical at times. Thoma Kunj cried like a child sitting close to Parvathy. He thought of Emily and experienced her presence; for him, Parvathy was evolving into his mother.

It took about six months for Thoma Kunj to recover from his depression, and he understood it was because of Parvathy that he regained himself. Thoma Kunj grew into a new man and expressed his desire to Parvathy and George Mooken to work in their pigsty. Soon, Thoma Kunj picked up his work and learned the techniques of castrating the piglets, about twenty to twenty-five of them every month. The rest of the time, he worked as a plumber, electrician and accountant for George Mooken.

Thoma Kunj renovated his house, built by Emily and Kurien. In the sitting room, he hung a large photograph of him sitting with his parents when he was about ten years old, just before his father's death. Before going to sleep, he talked to them eagerly, telling them what had happened that day and explaining each event. He could hear them talking to him, and the conversation continued for an hour.

Working with Parvathy and George Mooken was a joy; every night, Thoma Kunj looked forward to meeting them the following day. Except on festival days like Onam and Christmas, he excused himself from not eating with them even though they insisted on having food every day. He wanted to be independent, experiencing his freedom and silence.

Thoma Kunj cherished their company as they loved, respected and trusted him.

It was a Sunday morning. "Thoma Kunj," it was a voice he had been waiting for, for months together. Standing in the courtyard, looking at Thoma Kunj, Ambika's eyes filled with happiness.

"I wanted to come and visit. Every day I think about you, and I feel an emptiness. On my way to school, many days, I looked for you. Why did you stop going to school? My heart was heavy after not meeting you for many days. Please come back to school," Ambika said many things and struggled for breath, but her face projected hope.

"Ambika, I was not well. But every day I thought about you. I am so happy to meet you," he replied.

"Why don't you return to school?"

"I have been rusticated. I am no more a student. The headmaster refused to give me a transfer certificate to join another school," said Thoma Kunj. His words were clear and soft, without hatred or revenge.

Ambika looked at him in surprise as if she could not believe what she had heard. There was a sudden burst of emotions. He could see her sobbing, expressing her grief.

"Thoma Kunj, I love you. When I grow up, I want to marry you," Ambika said, looking into his eyes. The truth came from her soul and throbbed like her heart. For the first time, she talked about love, that too without formality, in plain words.

"I, too, love you, Ambika. I think of you often. I dreamt both of us swimming across the river together." Thoma Kunj said it slowly, looking into her eyes.

"I will wait for you, you alone," she said when she left.

Suddenly, someone touched Thoma Kunj, a hand that was the most powerful, sturdy and, at the same time, more caring he had ever experienced, other than his parents. The hand of God. He sensed it vividly as the hand gently led him to the final destination, under the gallows. He had been waiting for that hand for many years, nay for eternity. His mind was agitated for a second, but he tried to listen to the voices around him even though quietness pervaded everywhere. It was like a sensation of electric current flowing from the finger of the infinite and returning to his body. Mesmerised by the proximity of eternity, a once-in-a-lifetime experience,

Thoma Kunj looked at himself. It was the creation experience, the beginning of the universe, the emergence of a new Adam from the clay, like a potter shaping a pot, soothing, gentle and all-pervading. He was the man expelled from Eden to the darkness of prison. He was the innocent one who carried the crime on his shoulders like a cross to the Calvary. The hand that touched him was of the executioner, and Thoma Kunj knew it. God evolved into the hangman, and Thoma Kunj was the Christ, and he stepped forward, and his barefoot could sense the footrest of the gallows, which would be opened towards the pit when the lever was pulled. The footstep of the scaffold was smooth, and standing on it was like the supreme achievement after eleven years of waiting. It was the finality of one year of solitary confinement, waiting for the footsteps every day from three in the morning to five. There was a curiosity to touch and experience the gallows, to feel the roughness of the noose and dangling within the quarry. The hangman tied his legs, and he could sense the heaviness of his body but felt as if he was on the peak of Everest. The ligature around the legs was eternity's hug, gentle and soft but solid and inescapable.

But Ambika's first embrace was pleasant, creating exuberant lightning in every cell of his existence like the spread of a fierce fire on the hillside adjacent to Ayyankunnu forest.

"Thoma Kunj," she called. Fear was devouring her eyes.

"My father has arranged my marriage." Ambika was trembling. She was barely sixteen, in her first year at the higher secondary school after the tenth class. Ambika ran towards him as he was standing on the doorstep of his house.

She embraced him tightly and captured his lips within her mouth; her tongue ran over his cheeks and jaw like an infant heifer gulping the nipples and pressing its mother's udder with its nose. His vellus hairs, not so dark and coarse above his upper lips, cheeks and jaw, were wet with her saliva.

"Come in," she murmured while pulling him inside. It was for the first time Ambika was inside his house. She once again embraced him tightly and kissed his cheeks.

Her face and hands were swollen with a severe beating.

"My father is forcing me to marry someone whom I hate. He leads the Marxist party's youth wing revenge squad," Ambika said while bawling.

"Ambika," Thoma Kunj called her name repeatedly.

"We will run away from here. I want to live and die with you. My father thrashed me as I refused to consent to marry the devil; he chose for me. For a whole week, I was locked inside a room." Ambika's words were unclear, but they conveyed the deep distress she experienced.

"I am ready, Ambika, let us go to Virajpet, Gonikoppal or Madikeri. We can lead a happy life there. Come, we shall escape from this hell. But both of us are only sixteen and shall have to wait two more years to marry," Thoma Kunj replied, holding her hand and keeping her next to his chest. He could feel her tiny breast against his chest.

"Ambika!" There was a roar outside.

Thoma Kunj saw a group of men with hatchets and lathis. Two of them rushed inside. They pulled Ambika out of Thoma Kunj's hands.

"Bloody pig, you will suffer for your crime," Ambika's father shouted at Thoma Kunj while dragging his daughter.

"We will cut your head if you come after her. How will you look after her? You don't have even a moustache," a young man shouted, pointing his crude sword at the neck of Thoma Kunj.

"Thoma Kunj," Ambika's sobbing sounded like a murmur of tamarind leaves in the dusk before a storm.

The young man with the sword was the Education Minister of Kerala when Thoma Kunj walked toward the gallows, and Thoma Kunj knew not the same young man had hidden in a women's hostel room when Thoma Kunj went to repair the pipeline in the hostel.

The death penalty was an act to repay the rape and murder of a minor girl; whoever the killer, someone had to undergo the punishment. Or was it for embracing Ambika and reciprocating her love and trust? It might be for both. As incarceration was necessary, death on the gallows was inevitable; the innocent could wipe out the crime, the stain, and the sin. Death from a noose was poor compensation for rape, strangulation and murder, but death was a final recompense. Thoma Kunj could do nothing to the son of an MLA who became the education minister of God's Own country.

He felt the presence of another convict standing next to him and could sense his heavy breathing. The smell of a harem engulfed Thoma Kunj. There was the Mashrabiya, concubines in Abayas, Akeem searching for Razak with a scimitar in his right hand, and the blood-dripping sliced head of the Egyptian in his left.

"Is it you, Thoma Kunj?" was a faint voice. Thoma Kunj immediately recognised the voice.

"Razak," Thoma Kunj whispered.

"I pierced her and her paramour with a spear, like the spear of Akeem. The spike went through the hearts; she was four-month pregnant," Razak's voice was feeble.

"But..." Thoma Kunj could not complete his sentence.

"Akeem possessed me. The killing had a sexual fulfilment, the joy of a castrated man. I was in another prison that had no gallows. I reached here last night."

"Razak, I am sorry," Thoma Kunj whispered.

"This is the accomplishment of my life; I can show Padachon I can exist without him. I don't need seventy-two houris," Razak murmured.

Abruptly, Thoma Kunj heard the voice of the district magistrate; he was reading the warrant. The first was that of Razak's, then Thoma Kunj's.

Someone whispered in Thoma Kunj's ear: "Sorry, brother, I am doing my duty."

Thoma Kunj could sense the noose around his neck, and the executioner tightened it within a few seconds. The knot was against his throat so Thoma Kunj could die instantly without pain, breaking his spinal cord. He was a piglet; he heard the screeching of his sibling piggies as the executioner was pushing their heads within the abattoir, many thousands of them, and it was as if the encounter of dark monsoon clouds over the coffee plantations of Deva Moily. The soldier stood before George Mooken, lying on the floor with his double-barrelled gun, ready to scatter into smithereens the head of his daughter's husband. The shrieking sounded like the terrifying cry of Mohammed Akeem, holding a sword dripping with the blood of the Egyptian concubine:

"Allah, I will cut the head of the Mulhid."

Then there was the vision. The judge appeared before Thoma Kunj. Around sixty, he had flowing silver hair. Standing close to Thoma Kunj, and purred:

"You are my son, my only son. I am pleased with you." His voice was like the whistle of a train.

"No, you cannot be my father," Thoma Kunj opened his heart.

"Son, I loved you so much. I was testing you in this world to have eternal life in the next," the judge tried to cajole Thoma Kunj, rationalising his actions.

"You are wicked; you tortured my Mama. For you, only your life is precious, you do everything for your pleasure, and your decisions are always final," Thoma Kunj shouted. He wondered where he got the courage to confront the judge.

"Please accept me as your father," the judge pleaded.

"Kurien is my father, Emily, my mother. Go away, get lost in hell," Thoma Kunj screamed. His voice reverberated everywhere like a cyclone over the Arabian Sea.

The whole world trembled as if there was thunder and a thousand lightning. Thoma Kunj could sense the falling of the granite cross in front of the Ayyankunnu church. It broke into three equal pieces.

Ambika was talking to him; she looked lovely, like the morning mist over the Brahmagiri. They were somewhere in Kodagu, amid their coffee plantation, and Ambika sat with Thoma Kunj on a sofa built by him with teak wood. The lovely aroma of filter coffee permeated the balcony. He loved its smell and enjoyed the presence of his wife; she looked at him and smiled. Their children played in the courtyard, three of them, all girls.

There was a coup d'état in the paradise. As far outnumbered, the houris liberated heaven from Allah and the faithful male believers, pushing them into al-jahim bereft of women for sexual pleasure. There was the Egyptian woman with the severed head of Muhammad Akeem at the exit gate of paradise.

Unexpectedly Thoma Kunj heard the last cry of Razak. It was like a fierce sandstorm in the Arabian desert:

"Amira."

www.ingramcontent.com/pod-product-compliance
Lightning Source LLC
Chambersburg PA
CBHW051256250726
48656CB00004B/1314